Political Theology and International Law

International Legal Theory and Practice

Volumes published in this Brill Research Perspectives title are listed at *brill.com/rplt*

Political Theology and International Law

By

John D. Haskell

BRILL

LEIDEN | BOSTON

Originally published as Volume 1.2 (2018), in *International Legal Theory and Practice*, DOI:10.1163/24522058-01020002.

The Library of Congress Cataloging-in-Publication Data is available online at http://catalog.loc.gov
LC record available at http://lccn.loc.gov/2018954511

Typeface for the Latin, Greek, and Cyrillic scripts: "Brill". See and download: brill.com/brill-typeface.

ISBN 978-90-04-38250-3 (paperback)
ISBN 978-90-04-38251-0 (e-book)

This book is printed on acid-free paper and produced in a sustainable manner.

for Richard and J. VanMierlo

Contents

Political Theology and International Law

John D. Haskell
University of Manchester School of Law

Abstract

Political Theology and International Law offers an account of the intellectual debates surrounding the term "political theology" in academic literature concerning international law. Beneath these differences is a shared tradition, or genre, within the literature that reinforces particular styles of characterising and engaging predicaments in global politics. The text develops an argument toward another way of thinking about what political theology might offer international law scholarship – a politics of truth.

Keywords

Carl Schmitt – international legal theory – political theology – post-secularism

Acknowledgement

The text is part of a larger set of thoughts that began some time ago and continue through the present. Like most works of this sort, it is the outcome of many conversations and the support of colleagues, family and friends. I am especially grateful to David Kennedy, Scott Newton, and Akbar Rasulov. To name only a few of the many others that I am thankful to along the way in writing: Jean d'Aspremont, Justin Desautels-Stein, Jessica Fish, Peter Fitzpatrick, Rohan Grey, Martti Koskenniemi, Martha McCluskey, Mark Modak-Truran, Umut Özsu, Frank Pasquale, Nikolas Rajkovic, Pamela Slotte, and Jim Rosenblatt. The text reflects, perhaps more than anything, those many late night conversations with my father and I could not have asked for a closer friend through every step. And of course, though new to this world, Anna seems part of everything.

 | DOI:10.1163/9789004382510_002

1 Introduction

> There is always an alternative to the faith we lose. Or is it the same faith under another mask?
>
> GRAHAM GREENE, *The Comedians* (1966)

Turning into the 21st century the hour of religious kitsch seemed nigh, descending upon us from all sides. At the bookstores, shelves for the public geared to personal religious devotionals and spiritual guidance, explanations of politics through the prism of religious faith. On the television and internet, stories of violence in the name of God, fanaticism creeping into government policy from abroad and at home. In university classrooms, religion was no longer the domain of anthropology, history and religious studies but a respectable if not necessary point of investigation for students concerned with the contemporary world of international law and politics.[1] And a return to religious consideration in even the most unlikely of communities, Continental intellectuals who would have seemed securely secular (if not militantly atheistic) in posture suddenly appeared to be abandoning ship in search of some spiritually oriented framework.[2] What seems to unite these various conversations was a tacit agreement that the Enlightenment traditions of reason and Modernist emphasis on subjectivity felt at once parochial and passé. If 20th century international lawyers had staked their identity on transcending the irrationalities of religion and empire, the 21st century international lawyer now found legitimacy by rediscovering the religious dimensions of the profession's development. To be hip and relevant meant speaking of governance and meaning

1 "The Pope-mobile is everywhere, French youngsters lining up for a blessing, Russia as religious as Arkansas, a missionary energy in the third world rivaling the late 19th century, while here at home, Jesus on the Internet, alongside cults and chatroom confessionals. Children kneeling outside their schoolrooms, huddled like smokers on coffee break, begging just one quick nondenominational prayer. And then, of course, there is Islam, increasingly the modern figure of religion ... There is a thrill here ..." David Kennedy, "Losing Faith in the Secular: Law, Religion, and the Culture of International Governance" in Mark Janis and Carolyn Evans (eds), *Religion and International Law* (Kluwer 1999) (hereafter, Janis and Evans) 115.

2 See William Breckman, "Between Disenchantment and Political Theology: French Post-Marxism and the Return of Religion" 94 *New German Critique* 72 (2005); Michael Scott Christofferson, *French Intellectuals Against the Left: The Antitotalitarian Moment of the 1970s* (Berghahn Books 2004). Though Marxist activists have long been engaged in a religious frame of mind (e.g., 1950s and 60s liberation theology in Latin America), "secular" Marxist thinkers have in more recent years joined the fray to re-think the relationship between left oriented philosophy and Christian thought. For perhaps the most comprehensive study in this direction, see Roland Boer, *Criticism of Religion: On Marxism and Theology, II* (Brill 2009).

in the tongue of a "post-secular" world order.[3] In academic circles related to international law and political philosophy, the term "political theology" came to signal the dialogue around this sentiment.

The return of religion to sophisticated academic and governance talk implied that spiritual matters had been in some meaningful way absent, but this was never really the case.[4] For most of the 20th century, at least two intellectual traditions focused in on the relationship between religion and governance. First, Carl Schmitt symbolized the popular idea that conceptions of politics (and law) are secularized theological concepts.[5] And second, Leo Strauss would be identified for advancing the thesis that Christianity still mattered to the populations as a key ingredient of social cohesion among "Western" nation-states.[6]

---

3 For an elaborate effort in this mode, see Hent de Vries and Lawrence Sullivan (eds), *Political Theologies: Public Religions in a Post Secular World* (Fordham University Press 2006) (hereafter, de Vries and Sullivan). In relation to the meaning of "post-secular," see Peter Berger, Grace Davie and Effie Fokas (eds), *Religious America, Secular Europe? A Theme and Variation* (Routledge 2008); Jose Casanova, "Religion, European secular identities, and European integration" in Timothy Byrnes and Peter Katzenstein (eds), *Religion in an Expanding Europe* (Cambridge University Press 2006). For a helpful analysis on post-foundational thought at the crossroads of political theology and post-secularism that traces a lineage from the political philosophy of Weimar Germany (e.g., Heidegger, Schmitt) through the intellectual scene in post-WW2 France (e.g., Lefort) into the contestation between modern Marxist and post-Marxist voices (e.g., Badiou, Laclau), see Oliver Marchart, *Post-Foundational Political Thought: Political Difference in Nancy, Lefort, Badiou and Laclau* (Edinburgh University Press 2007).

4 See Nathaniel Berman, "The Sacred Conspiracy: Religion, Nationalism, and the Crisis of Internationalism" 25:1 *Leiden Journal of International Law* 9 (2012); John Haskell "Divine Immanence: The Evangelical Foundations of Modern Anglo-American Approaches to International Law" 11:3 *Chinese Journal of International Law* 429 (2012).

5 See Carl Schmitt, *Political Theology: Four Chapters on the Concept of Sovereignty* (originally published 1922; University of Chicago Press 2006). Schmitt has enjoyed a renaissance in academic thought over the past two decades with a number of his works translated into English and a proliferation of secondary literature authored especially within more "progressive" academic circles of philosophy, political science and international law. For example, see Matilda Arvidsson, Leila Brännström, and Panu Minkkinen (eds), *The Contemporary Relevance of Carl Schmitt: Law, Politics and Theology* (Routledge 2015); Mitchell Dean, "A Political Theology of World Order: Carl Schmitt's Nomos" 23:5 *Theory, Culture, and Society* 1 (2006); Martti Koskenniemi, "International Law as Political Theology: How to Read Nomos der Erde" 11:4 *Constellations* 492 (2004).

6 See Leo Strauss, *Natural Right and History* (University of Chicago Press 1953); Leo Strauss, "On the Interpretation of Genesis" 21:1 *L'Homme* 5 (1981). Discussing Strauss' belief that liberal democracy carried a necessary connection to a metaphysical moral order that was not rationally defensible, and providing citations to primary and secondary literature on this theme, see John Gray, *Black Mass: Apocalyptic Religion and the Death of Utopia* (Penguin Books 2006) 128–145. For a concise analysis of the linkage between Schmitt and Strauss in the wider context of Weimar anti-liberal thought and American political philosophy, see John P. McCormick, "Political Theory and Political Theology: The Second Wave of Carl Schmitt in English"

Both visions of Christianity's continued relevance operated on a formal level whereby God was not so much killed off as bracketed: for Schmitt, a structural explanation of political arrangements, and for Strauss, a function or strategy of wise governance.[7] This meant that while Christianity might not be something that could be necessarily escaped, it was fundamentally different than what they saw as the "pre-modern" era, in that it would have no role in shaping the substance of political/legal decisions.[8] The logic followed that if the state was a secularized version of the divine will, its leadership was in fact following the dictates of material interests and not Biblical scripture, religious organizations, or any internal voice of God. If policy makers had to invoke or listen to the religious beliefs of populations, it was for strategic political gain rather than any aligned faith-based commitment. Or, at most, one was a Christian the same way one wore a suit and tie to work – it was just the right thing to do.[9]

A paradox that rises then from these positions read together is that the loss of faith at once poses a potential grave threat to Western civilization and is a symbol of its progress toward a more cosmopolitan world order. After all,

---

26:6 *Political Theory* 830 (1998); William Connolly, "Pluralism and Faith" in de Vries and Sullivan, supra note 3 at 272.

7 There is a significant tendency in legal scholarship to analogize theological and legal subjects: God-State, Bible-Constitution, Believers-Populations, Priests-Judges, and so forth. Often, the discussion is framed to argue a spiritual dimension to democratic secular regimes – for instance, to describe the American political system as a civil religion, and to explain various institutional roles in a quasi-religious terminology. For example, see Paul Kahn, *A Political Theology for a Civil Religion*, Lecture at European University Institute Robert Schuman Centre for Advanced Studies (January 2012); Duncan Kennedy, "American Constitutionalism as Civil Religion: Notes of an Atheist" 19 *Nova Law Review* 909 (1995); Joseph Weiler, "Europe in Crisis – On Political Messianism, Legitimacy and the Rule of Law" *Singapore Journal of Legal Studies* 248 (2012). The analogy in these studies is usually wildly under-theorized, if not sloppily executed, especially in relation to authors' treatment of theology. For a more unexpected and fun stylistic variation, Nathaniel Berman plays with the idea of the past offering a set of practices and a mentality of (esoteric and exoteric) governance that engages in an almost supernatural preoccupation, what he equates with the "alchemy" of the medieval and Renaissance periods. Nathaniel Berman, *The Alchemy of Empire, or, of Power and Primitivism*, Inaugural Lecture of the School of Oriental and African Studies Centre for the study of Colonialism, Empire and International Law (February 2008) (transcript on file with author).

8 In the mid-to-late 20th century, civilization was often thought to have displaced religion as a central organizing trope in governance and social life. "In the new age, nationalism, taking the place of religion, was as diversified in its manifestations and aspirations, in its form and even in its substance as religion itself." Hans Kohn, *The Idea of Nationalism: A Study in its Origins and Background* (Macmillan 1944) 574.

9 An example of this type during the Cold War era may be seen in John Foster Dulles. See Bevan Sewell, "Pragmatism, Religion, and John Foster Dulles's Embrace of Christian Internationalism in the 1930s" 41:4 *Diplomatic History* 799 (2017).

Nazism and Communism were God-less regimes hell-bent on the overthrow of a liberal democratic way of life. To discard the idea of God did not lead to emancipation but a theology of cosmic horror. Encouraging personal faith is therefore its panacea, a doorway to cultural well-being and individual liberty. But the disruptions to international peace and stability since the dismemberment of the Soviet Union are characterized exactly by this re-embrace of religious meaning. The war on terror, the rise of fundamentalist Christianity, xenophobia within Western Europe toward Arab-speaking populations, the third wave liberal humanitarianism that gives lip service to religious equality while regularly branding non-Christian behavior as ignorant or barbaric[10] ... Religious passion seems fundamentally part of the problem.

The more international law scholarship concentrated on dilemmas in this register, the more it seemed to frustrate any governance posture. From one corner, the scholar should not ignore the Christian roots of the contemporary Western experience, and the more general spiritual dimensions of law and politics. There is no simple opting out of religion for an objective, rational perspective that might mediate conflicting passions. The return of confessional politics throughout the post-colonial space challenges the claimed non-partisan/non-confessional disposition of international law's cosmopolitan spirit, demanding international law to declare itself, to take a chance and go ahead, to be fanatical about something, anything.[11] Quit pretending you don't

10 For example, see Samuel Huntington, *The Clash of Civilisations and the Remaking of World Order* (Simon and Schuster 1996).

11 Speaking of the secular establishment of international law, David Kennedy gives voice to this sense of despair that is haunting the cosmopolitan claim to impartiality: "Everywhere there is ideology, politics, passion, but not here, among the reasonable men and women of the enlightenment, graced with infinite time, reason and the modesty of the truly powerful. But some days it's just not enough. Terror and nation and fundament, held firmly at bay, shame us, mock us – how long can we inhabit the high road of cultural denial when we know that we too stand for something dammit. It's not just the Sudanese and Chinese and Sinhalese who have roots and religion." See Kennedy, supra note 1 at 125. In this sense, the irony of the anti-totalitarian rhetoric within "progressive" blocs of Western academia is that its participants are not repulsed by violent acts and authoritarian rituals (after all, we fantasize about this in movies, in wagering salaries at casinos or the stock market, when we gamble with our health smoking), but intimates that the attraction to speaking about violence is possibly about – to some degree – a conjured nostalgia and implicit desire to experience the adventure that our ancestors must have felt in staking out the Western order. This seems to me a distinctly Christian preoccupation, to pretend that we can confess our guilt and be done with it, without any real penitence. The anxiety of influence here is not that we are unable to evade the horrors of our ancestors, that their sins may shame us, but the fear that we might not live up to the stature and success of our dead forbearers, and the perverse pleasure we secretly harbour in the privileges of rulership. This may be partly what David Kennedy is getting at when he urges humanitarians

have a master and admit your God. From another equally valid corner, however, spirituality with any sort of meaningfulness, with some teeth, seems to easily get out of hand and requires some sort of moderating all-too-humanist influence. We wanted you to go to Sunday school, but don't take the stories too seriously or make polite society uncomfortable. No matter where we look, choices appear precarious. The turn to political theology did not ultimately offer the escape we might have hoped for.

To make matters worse for the field, the global crisis of the last decade effectively re-centred scholarship on the economy. Political theology swung to political economy. Saving one's mortgage felt more pressing than saving one's soul. This is not to say that political theology literature does not continue to be produced (it does, and in productive ways),[12] but the field suddenly looks dormant in comparison to 10 or 20 years ago – much like political economy literature back in the 80s and 90s played a distant second fiddle to scholarship oriented around cultural studies and philosophically deconstructed individuality.[13] The actors and institutions geared around terrorism have not abated, they are now just incorporated into a broader story of market instability and financial insecurity. In such a climate, it seems easy to dismiss political theology literature as a product of those glory days before we realized it was actually always all about capitalism.

By contrast, the text here is all about political theology in relation to international law, and it deliberately taps into the style and substance of those debates that until quite recently seemed the rage in the academy. My interest is not to call for resuscitating political theology literature in international law or to minimize the benefit of thinking about governance as a problem of capitalism, but rather to try and capture some of what that moment was about and reflect on what it tells us about the discipline moving forward. The conclusion draws this thinking together to argue for what we might call a "politics of truth." Throughout the text, political theology might be most usefully viewed as a rhetorical mechanism, or species of disciplinary sub-genre, that generates certain types of arguments in an attempt to reconcile anxiety-producing contradictions that animate the various doctrinal positions and thematic of international law

to "recapture[e] a politics of war" where they may feel "the weight and the lightness of killing or allowing to live." David Kennedy, *Of War and Law* (Princeton University Press 2006) 171. For a classic statement about the anxiety of influence, see Harold Bloom, *The Anxiety of Influence: A Theory of Poetry* (Oxford University Press 1973).

12 For a recent discussion specifically related to law from a theological orientation, see Helge Årsheim and Pamela Slotte, *The Juridification of Religion* (Brill 2017).

13 See Elizabeth Clark, *History, Theory, Text: Historians and the Linguistic Turn* (Harvard University Press 2004).

itself – or even more modest, not of international law broadly, but simply those of us who identify as international law academics.[14] To put my own cards on the table, at least within the English speaking academy, Christianity molds our professional roles and vocabularies, with even our most heterodox colleagues expressing religious fidelity.[15] The challenge is not escape, but play.[16]

2 A Christian Heritage in Perilous Times

The recourse to religion and spirituality within international law scholarship is commonly premised on a feeling of existential crisis,[17] though scholars agonize

---

14 For discussions around this general theme, see David Kennedy, "When Renewal Repeats: Thinking Against the Box" 32 *New York Journal of International Law and Politics* 335 (2000).

15 For the suggestion that international law suppresses a Christian ambivalence toward its history with Jewish people, see Reut Paz, *A Gateway between a Distant God and a Cruel World: The Contribution of Jewish German-Speaking Scholars to International Law* (Brill 2012). For an argument that legal academics think about law in the shadow of classical theological proofs of God, see Pierre Schlag, "Law as a Continuation of God by Other Means" 85 *California Law Review* 427 (1997). From a Marxist position, positioning Christianity not as opiate but a constitutive factor of bourgeois ideology, especially in the composition of the liberal, democratic (atheist) nation state, see Alberto Toscano, "Beyond Abstraction: Marx and the Critique of the Critique of Religion" 18:1 *Historical Materialism* 3 (2010); Warren Breckman, *Marx, The Young Hegelians, and the Origins of Radical Social Theory* (Cambridge University Press 1999) 294–295. To foreground an argument that will develop in the text, critiques about capitalist and/or Christian alienation that might otherwise encourage a collective disjunction with the prevailing order are transformed to represent perennial conditions of thought for all humanity whereby any challenge is muted to ultimately justify the tradition it originally seemed set to critique. In other words, we move from structural redistribution and political rupture to social engagement that is ameliorative and consensual. For a discussion circling these themes, see John Roberts, "The 'Returns to Religion:' Messianism, Christianity and the Revolutionary Tradition. Part I: Wakefulness to the Future" 16 *Historical Materialism* 59 (2008), and "Part II: The Pauline Tradition" 16 *Historical Materialism* 77 (2008).

16 And by play, to be aware to the treachery of language and to dare concrete direct action, to be bold. On this theme, see Grace Lee, "David Lynch: The Treachery of Language," available at https://www.youtube.com/watch?time_continue=639&v=fllV6-aqWU.

17 The distinction between the political and politics can be traced back to Weimar German political theorists, and is later picked up by post-Marxist French intellectuals. The "political" designates a "broadly shared political framework or public space," what Ricoeur would describe as an ideal sphere that could claim to embody some rational concord, whereas "politics" signifies the "pursuit of partisan strategies or programs." See Marchart, supra note 4 at 4–5, 36–59 (quoting Fred Dallmayr and exploring two distinct traditions, the "Arendtians" and the "Schmittians"). What runs through variations on this theme is some sense that while politics signifies the everyday struggles within a given order over

about its nature and how to respond.[18] On the one hand, a significant strand of scholarship views the loss of a Christian foundation ushering in immanent political nihilism. On the other hand, a substantial scholarship finds any mode of simple rationality too thin to sustain community and order, and argues for a new vocabulary of governance that can only be understood through Christian thought but emptied of its substantive message. Often the advocates of the first position profess some confessional faith, while authors writing from the second position tend towards a more agnostic position that forswears any hint of conventional religious creed or dogma (though may emphasize the need for some mysticism). Aside from the relatively isolated – albeit vocal – pockets of militant atheism that claim religion is a black and white category of ignorance and evil, what these two positions hold in common is the sense that the legacy of Christianity offers the promise of resurrection and new life for an ageing Western culture.[19]

If we allow ourselves a slight detour, this sentiment is evidently part of an older intellectual traditional pervasive in different forms throughout Western Europe and North America, closely linked to the age of colonialism and empire: the belief that the success of the nation (or Western culture) rides on

---

social power, access to resources and so on, the political is the rare moment of rupture and foundation-making.

18 See Dean, supra note 5.

19 Richard Dawkins and Daniel Dennett, for instance, advance the virtues of a militant atheism over what is seen as the dangerous ignorance implicit in religious faith. Adherents to religions of all stripes, writes Dennett, "put at risk what we hold dear...." See Daniel Dennett, *Breaking the Spell: Religion as a Natural Phenomenon* (Penguin Books 2006); Richard Dawkins, *The God Delusion* (Transworld Publishers 2006). While comedian and talk show host Bill Maher has made popular this line of attack to American movie-going audiences (in his 2007 documentary, *Religulous*), more subdued variations of it also enter the political and legal mainstream (it is unclear to what extent they might target Christian faiths as well if politically expedient): for instance, in the visible discomfort displayed by European courts towards female Muslim headscarves and the call among British politicians for a wholesale social education policy in "British-ness," which not so subtlety targets Islamic populations in need of indoctrination. These sentiments find their way into even more left-liberal legal scholars. "While the Catholic Church and Islam can claim an engagement with international human rights issues on some issues, they have played a negative and problematic role in other human rights contexts. The issue that has most often provoked this reaction is that of women's rights and it has fostered a striking and incongruous alliance between the two religious traditions. A coalition of the Islamic countries, the Holy See ... and some Catholic countries has been the most prominent in the 1990s ..." Hilary Charlesworth, "The Challenges of Human Rights Law for Religious Traditions" in Janis and Evans, supra note 2 at 406–407.

its faithfulness to a divine covenant.[20] In 1889, for instance, the first hymn book was released that contained an entire section explicitly devoted to national hymns of Britain, and it was not uncommon to see congregations across denominations singing praises to the empire, a sort of "Spiritual Israel:"

> Our bounds of empire though hast set in many a distant isle
> And in the shadow of our throne the desert places smile
> For in our laws and in our faith it's thine own light they see
> The truth that brings to captive souls the wider liberty.[21]

Similarly, in France, the religious revival of the early 1870s inspired thousands of men and women to Catholic shrines, and prophets announced the vision of the Pope and French Emperor ruling together over Europe and the colonial landscape. Writing in this spirit, the prominent 19th century French historian, Jules Michelet, would celebrate the unique calling of the French in almost apocalyptic tones:

> No doubt every great nation represents an idea important to the human race. But great God! How much more true is this of France! Suppose for a moment that she were eclipsed or perished; the sympathetic bond of the world would be loosened, broken, and probably destroyed. Love, which is the life of the world, would be wounded in its most vital part. The earth would enter into an age of ice which other world nearby have already entered.[22]

In the United States, this sentiment dated back to the first settler colonies on the Eastern seaboard, but with an interesting twist. While undoubtedly coloured by nationalist rhetoric, the liberal establishment tended to see the American experience indelibly tied to its European heritage and sought to promote a spiritual sense of brotherhood that would justify its colonial efforts, but

20 "[A]ll nations ... have long agreed that they are chosen peoples; the idea of special destiny is as old as nationalism itself." Russell Nye, *The Almost Chosen People* (Michigan State University Press 1966) 164; William Hutchison and Hartmutt Lehmann (eds), *Many are Chosen: Divine Election and Western Nationalism* (Fortress Press 1994) (hereafter Hutchison and Lehmann).

21 See A.F. Walls, "Carrying the White Man's Burden: Some British Views on National Vocation in the Imperial Era" in Hutchison and Lehmann, supra note 20 at 44–46.

22 Quoted by Thomas Kselman, "Religion and French Identity: The Origins of the Union Sacree" in Hutchison and Lehmann, supra note 20 at 60. For a study of Jules Michelet in context, see Roland Barthes, *Michelet* (originally published 1954, University of California Press 1992).

with the necessary caveat that no one nation could claim to rule the world – in fact, it was a symbol of progress and providential desire towards liberal democratic/republican rule that many nations could now be the voice of history at once, usually embodied in some "Anglo-Saxon" ideal.[23] Writing in 1886, the famous Congregational clergyman Josiah Strong would sum up this belief:

> It seems to me that God with infinite wisdom and skill is training the AngloSaxon race for an hour sure to come in the world's future ... the final competition of races for which the Anglo-Saxon is being schooled ... [and] this race of unequaled energy, with all the majesty of numbers and the might of wealth behind it – the representatives, let us hope, of the largest liberty, the purest Christianity, the highest civilization – having developed peculiarly aggressive traits calculated to impress its institutions upon mankind will spread itself over the earth ... Can anyone doubt that the result of this competition of races will be the survival of the fittest ... Is there any reasonable doubt that this race ... is destined to dispossess many weaker races, assimilate them, and model the remainder, until, in a very real sense, it has Anglo-Saxonized mankind?[24]

At least three claims are being made here which would find salience in the horrors of 20th century European society. First, the political hegemony of Western

23 Perhaps the most classic expression of this idea in the American legal tradition comes from Supreme Court Justice John Marshall in the case *Johnson v. McIntosh*, 21 U.S. (8 Wheat.) 543 (1823). "The discovery of this immense continent, the great nations of Europe were eager to appropriate to themselves so much of it as they could respectively acquire. Its vast extent offered an ample field to the ambition and enterprise of all; and the character and religion of its inhabitants afforded an apology for considering them as a people over whom the superior genius of Europe might claim an ascendency. The potentates of the old world found no difficulty in convincing themselves that they made ample compensation to the inhabitants of the new, by bestowing on them civilization and Christianity, in exchange for unlimited independence ... [A]s they were all in pursuit of nearly the same object, it was necessary, in order to avoid conflicting settlements, and consequent war with each other, to establish a principle, which all should acknowledge as the law by which the right of acquisition, which they all asserted, should be regulated as between themselves. This principle was, that discovery gave title to the government by whose subjects, or by whose authority, it was made, against all other European governments, which title might be consummated by possession. The exclusion of all other Europeans, necessarily gave to the nation making the discovery the sole right of acquiring the soil from the natives, and establishing settlements upon it. It was a right with which no Europeans could interfere. It was a right which all asserted for themselves, and to the assertion of which, by others, all assented."

24 Josiah Strong, *Our Country: Its Possible Future and Its Present Crisis* (The American Home Missionary Society 1885) 174–175.

nation-states is a symbol of their "chosen-ness" and proves the supremacy of their institutional arrangements and value-systems. Second, these nation-states are unified around a common "natural" characteristic (the "AngloSaxon race"). And third, their religious calling (promoting "the largest liberty, the purest Christianity, the highest civilization") nevertheless operates within a cruel, Darwinist world where those who cannot rise to the challenges and standards of freedom will face annihilation or assimilation. It is not too difficult to see the logic that would allow for the Nazi extermination camps striving to bring forth a "new man." There is a deeply Christian logic to the entire process: if the death of Jesus (the "King of the Jews") was required to inaugurate the Pauline "new man" of Gentile Christians, the collective murder of the Jewish people would not only right their original sin of executing the Son of God, but stand in as a modern day sacrifice that might enable a new "messianic" race to emerge from the ashes of a faltering European culture after the storms of the Second World War. But intimations of this genealogy also ground contemporary international law arguments, especially when authors appeal to some spiritual essence that might hold off the tides of anarchy.

Take for instance the work of the late Harold Berman, who helped inaugurate the law and religion movement in American academia and argued forcefully for international law to embrace its Christian heritage.[25] Describing the nature of the crisis at the doors of the West, he writes:

> Western man is undergoing an integrity crisis – the kind of crisis that many individual men and women experience in their early fifties when they ask themselves with utmost seriousness, and often in panic, what

25 To date, there is little work on the epistemological/sociological development of law and religion scholarship. But see John Witte, Jr., *Religion and Law*, Interview on University of California Television Conversations with History (August 2011), available at https://www.youtube.com/watch?v=W5glYC_topE. Though only speculative, the rise of law and religion scholarship may begin in the mid-20th century with the marriage between evangelical white America and capitalist elite wary of democratic excess. There is a growing literature engaged in various facets of this general alliance, such as William Leach, *Land of Desire: Merchants, Power, and the Rise of a New American Culture* (Random House 1993); Nancy MacLean, *Democracy in Chains: The Deep History of the Radical Right's Stealth Plan for America* (Viking Press 2017); Michael McVicar, *Christian Reconstruction: R.J. Rushdoony and American Religious Conservatism* (University of North Carolina Press 2015); Bethany Moreton, *To Serve God and Wal-Mart: The Making of the Christian Free Enterprise* (Harvard University Press 2009).

> their lives have stood for and where they are headed ... Our whole culture seems to be facing the possibility of a kind of nervous breakdown.[26]

For Berman, the stakes are high, because unlike an "identity crisis" that might relate to the transition from youth to adulthood, an "integrity crisis" signals the "closure" of the whole life cycle, what Erik Erikson describes as "the despair of the knowledge that a limited life is coming to a conscious conclusion" and that seeks to counter this despair with "some world order and spiritual sense, no matter how dearly paid for."[27] The symptoms of this despair, in Berman's view, are located in the popular "loss of confidence in religion and in law" rising from the First World War and with a "deeper loss of confidence in fundamental religious and legal values, a decline of belief in the commitment to any kind of transcendent reality that gives life meaning, and a decline of belief in and commitment to any structures and processes that provide social order and social justice."[28] Here, the tragedy is that the decline of the law signals the very undoing of what he sees as the democratic character of Western society itself, with its emphasis on the rule of law as a restraint against the arbitrary will of the sovereign or the anarchism of the mob:

> People must feel that it is their law, or they will not respect it. But they will only have that feeling when the law, through its rituals and traditions and through its authority and its universality, touches and evokes their sense of the whole of life, their sense of ultimate purpose, their sense of the sacred ... To quote the language of the founder of the historical school of jurisprudence, the great nineteenth century German jurist Friedrich Karl von Savigny, this is a body of law that is developed "first by custom and by popular belief, then by juristic activity – everywhere, therefore, by internal, silently operating forces, not by the arbitrary will of a legislator" ... [Despite changes] the Western legal tradition still bears the marks of its origins ... for the belief that so long as law remains autonomous, so long as it conforms to reason and morality, so long as it develops and grows to

---

26 Harold Berman, *Faith and Order: The Reconciliation of Law and Religion* (Scholars Press 1993). Berman wrote extensively on the historical and theoretical relationship between law and religion. I have limited the conversation here to this single book, as it was published late in his life and is a collection of his essays and speeches over the course of two decades concerning various historical and contemporary themes about the engagement of law and religion, with a specifically global perspective.

27 Id. at 2 (quoting Erik Erikson). See Erik Erikson, *Childhood and Society* (Imago Publishing 1951) and *Insight and Responsibility* (Norton and Company 1964).

28 Id. at ix, 15, 284.

> meet new challenges, it will continue to be able to resolve individual and social conflicts and to maintain order and justice.[29]

This growing cynicism to law's promise of participatory justice and order is the consequence of four socio-historical shifts. First, the legacy of the Reformation unduly separated the religious (moral) and political (civil) aspects of authority, leading students into the traps of "rule formalism, on one hand, and political power on the other."[30] Second, in step with this earlier division between religion and politics/law, the 20th century horrors of war and the shame of colonialism have led to the idea of law solely as a body of formal pragmatic rules aimed to achieve specified political agendas, thereby turning law into a soulless, bureaucratic machinery that is ever-more "fragmented, more subjective, geared more to expediency and less to morality, concerned more with immediate consequences and less with consistency or continuity."[31] Third, just as the law is now fractured, so to the underlying community that gives it life. For Berman, the divisions "of race, of class, of the sexes, and of the generations" have supplanted the "true religious foundations of Western law ... the populus Christianus," and in doing so, "weak[ened] ... bonds of kinship and of soil."[32] Fourth, lawyers (and Western populations more generally) have lost sight

29 Id. at 14, 45, 283.

30 "I must take issue with the neo-Lutheran emphasis on the sharp separation of Law and Gospel, law and grace, law and creativity, which led the 19th century German to extreme legal conceptualism and to the positivist reduction of law to a system of rules enacted by the state." Id. at 330.

31 Id. at 39.

32 Id. at 6–7. The implications of this claim are disconcerting, but a widely shared sentiment among many in intellectual legal circles. For versions of this theme in a slightly different register, see William Bennett, *Why We Fight: Moral Clarity and the War on Terrorism* (Doubleday 2003) and Samuel Huntington, *Who We Are: The Challenges to America's National Identity* (Simon and Schuster 2004). We should be clear about Berman's claim being made here: the Western legal order is tied to a particular Christian community that arose sometime between the 12th and 16th centuries, and that these links between past generations and the future stability and prosperity of the West are held together by ties to blood and soil. If we recall, however, the formation of the Western legal order was built on the back of violent exclusion (e.g., genocide, population transfers) and liberal nation-states subsequently organized themselves, in part, through a collective amnesia. For a study into some of these themes, see Umut Özsu, *Formalizing Displacement: International Law and Population Transfers* (Oxford University Press 2015). This exclusionary thinking found resonance in the racial policies during the colonial experience and again, on a more systematic scale, with the Nazis. The blood involved in these ties between the past, present and future are not simply genealogical, but the very real death and suffering of untold millions as the collateral damage and object of organized brutality in constructing our current dispensation. My point here is not to condemn the Western experience, but

of the divine Providence at work in Western history, and in turn, are increasingly unwilling to partake in a theory of justice that would transcend individual egotisms to lead society towards greater unity and higher moral standards of justice and love:[33]

> Contemporary social science characterizes modern law by the words "secular" and "rational." The alleged secularism of law is linked with the decline of the belief in either a divine law or a divinely inspired natural law. The law of the modern state, it is said, is not a reflection of any sense of ultimate meaning and purpose in life; instead, its tasks are finite, material, impersonal – to get things done, to make people act in certain ways ... If law is merely an experiment, and if judicial decisions are only hunches, why should individuals or groups of people observe those legal rules or commands that do not conform to their interests?[34]

This apathy and fragmentation is a threat to human affairs, but also our collective spiritual future:

> ... the study of law cannot be treated by us as a purely "academic" matter. When we approach law as believers we must understand it as part of God's plan of salvation. We know that our mission goes beyond the law, but we also know that by this faith we do not overthrow the law. By no means, on the contrary, we uphold the law. We uphold it as a means of preparing our hearts and minds to receive faith and to grow in hope and love ... It was in the West, and I believe it was only in the West, that

---

to hesitate before we wax romantic. See Peter Danchin, "The Emergence and Structure of Religious Freedom in International Law Reconsidered" 23 *Journal of Law and Religion* 455 (2008).

33 That secularism and rationality lead to the alienation of the community and the law is, in Berman's view, closely related to what he sees as the turn to Soviet-style "collectivism." "In part, the crisis of legal education is due to the radical centralization and bureaucratization of economic life, of which socialism in one form or another is an aspect or a consequence ... We have moved from an individualistic to a collectivistic age." Berman, supra note 26 at 339. This seems to contradict his earlier arguments that the foundation of law is rooted in collective religious communities, but which also becomes more understandable if we read his argument in the tradition of Carl Schmitt. Schmitt felt Western culture (rooted in ancient Christian community) was haunted by the bureaucratization of law, its greatest threat coming from the Soviet Union, which he saw as the Anti-Christ made flesh, and hence the need for the "katechontic restrainer" (once the Church, and for Schmitt, now vested in the political sovereign). See Carl Schmitt, *The Nomos of the Earth in the International Law of the Jus Publicum Europaeum* (Telos 2003) 59–60.

34 Berman, supra note 26 at 6–7.

> the belief in the ongoing character of law was conceived and came to prevail ... [and] the Judaic Christian insight [is] that man is more than a natural phenomenon, more even than an observer of natural phenomena, that man is rather a creature of God who partakes also of God's creative powers ...[35]

Here, the law is fundamentally tied to a particular present community (Western Europe and America), but the law is equally autonomous from the particularities of geography and time to express a deeper moral truth, some natural, universal condition of human experience. The formal ideal of the nation-state, for Berman, embodies this tension: at once the historical product of a Western public international law capable of embodying the collective spirit of a particular community and also a formal ideal that always leaves open (transcends) any particular claim, pointing towards something beyond it. "[The] state itself ... derives its character as a state from its membership in the international community of states.... [Thus] to claim the right to govern and the right to defend or attack – to claim the authority of a 'state' – is to acknowledge participation in a legal order which transcends the state and which defines statehood."[36] Only the Western legal order captures a truly universal language, which opens up the possibility for a new age that demands a new subject: "Planetary Man ... [where] all inhabitants of Planet Earth share a common destiny."[37] The ambition is not to abandon the Christian heritage of international law, but to adopt it as the precondition for the future world order, for this heritage to seize the role of the New Adam, to name a new creation:

> This, indeed, is the crisis of our legal tradition: that we are at the end of one era and at the beginning of another. We are at the end of an era in which world history was centered in Western history and at the beginning of an era in which Western history is centered in world history ... [A] new global legal tradition is emerging which in some ways threatens the Western legal tradition at the same time that it, in some ways, builds upon it ... I believe that if we open our minds to the inspiration of the Holy Spirit and pray for his guidance in intellectual manners, we shall discover new truth ... For the truth is that God does not call us to be merely observers of life; rather he calls all of us – even the scholars – in all that we do – to participate with him in the process of spiritual death

35 Id. at 306.
36 Id. at 281.
37 Id. at 277, 286.

> and rebirth which is the fundamental religious experience ... The crucial question is, what kind of Man he or she are to be.[38]

To participate in this "process of spiritual death and rebirth" from the Western Man to the Planetary Man demands nothing less than international lawyers assume the role of priests, distilling the divine universal message hidden in both the text and history of public international law:

> God reveals himself both in nature and in man, and that therefore the study of natural and human phenomena will disclose God's purposes ... The claim upon a lawyer to think and act responsibly as a lawyer in helping to maintain unity within the society, resolve conflict, and allocate power – this, too, is a religious claim ... a priestly vocation, that is, a calling to play a part as responsible leaders in their communities. In the Western political tradition and especially in that of the United States, the legal profession constitutes a secular priesthood.[39]

At first glance, Berman's open call for international lawyers to see themselves as a priesthood (re)committed to a Christian heritage and international law acting as a ladder between humanity and God sets him out as a relatively extraordinary figure for a professional culture marked by its professed agnosticism toward religious faith.[40] Dig deeper though, and his apology for Western Christendom looks familiar to mainstream cosmopolitan positions. Liberal voices may often be more timid to proclaim any denominational tradition or creed for inspiration, but they tend to reiterate the idea that public international law embodies values that are universal, or the direct product of the Western legal tradition, or even go so far as to paint international law in religious terms.

The cause of human rights in international law, for instance, is often characterized to mimic the missionary zeal of Christianity, the doctrines of international law "a sort of revealed truth:"[41]

> International lawyers share an appealing evangelistic, even messianic, agenda. We are on a mission to improve the human condition. For many, perhaps most of us, this mission requires preferring the international

38 Id. at 286, 309, 321–22.

39 Id. at 351. For a discussion of this theme among 19th century international lawyers, see Haskell, supra note 4.

40 See Paz, supra note 4 at xvii.

41 See Tawia Ansah, "A Terrible Purity: International Law, Morality, Religion, Exclusion" 38:1 *Cornell International Law Journal* 9 (2005) (quoting Mark Weisburg).

> "over the nation, integration over sovereignty." Multilateralism is our shared secular religion. Despite all or our disappointments with its functioning, we still worship at the shrine of global institutions like the UN.[42]

These authors tend to share with Berman a sense of horror at the growing bureaucratic, technocratic creep into the virtue of the law – what the Finnish diplomat and European legal philosopher, Martti Koskenniemi, characterizes as the "police ... ransacking the temple:"

> The police are ransacking the temple, searching for criminals and those it call terrorists. The mind of the police – the security police in this case – is a machine, programmed to believe that history ended and we won it; that what remains is a clash of civilizations and we intend to come up first. As it proceeds – helmets, boots, blackjacks and all – towards the altar, the people draw silently away into the small chapels, surrounding the navis, each to attend communion before a different god. After the police have gone, the altar hall is empty but for the few that were left to guard it, and their admirers. The frescoes, the bronze statuettes, the stained glass, the marble speak from different ages, through different symbols, and towards a now empty centre ... The peace of the police is not the calm of the temple but the silence of the tomb.[43]

This is a passionate appeal against what he sees to be the armies of bureaucrats and soldiers overthrowing the tradition of the Western legal order (and particularly the General Assembly of the United Nations), a melancholic picture framed in Christian tropes set against the horrors of 20th century warfare: on the one side, "the security police," of "helmets, boots, [and] blackjacks," and on the other side, fleeing from the advancing soulless "programmed ... machine," the "people" silently drawing into "small chapels," surrounding the "navis," leaving behind the "alter" with its baroque symbols of Christian faith and universal love. If Alvarez sees hope in human rights, Koskenniemi tends to adopt a vision that borders on despair, though never quite succumbing. The temple possesses the silence of a tomb, but it stands waiting for the faithful to return. For Nathaniel Berman, it is precisely these dispossessed adherents of a cosmopolitan internationalism (the paradoxical nature of passionate national identity and the desire for universal peace) – keeping faith in the future return

42 Id. at 39 (quoting José Alvarez).

43 Martti Koskenniemi, "The Police in the Temple: Order, Justice and the UN: A Dialectical View" 6 *European Journal of International Law* 25 (2004).

to the temple – that constitute the spiritual vanguard against the ambition of empire and the barbarity of terrorism:

> I urge those who continue to believe in peace neither to give in to the faith of the assassins and bombers, nor to seek refuge in the sterile rationalism which is doomed to abstractly condemn what it cannot understand … Only those who have felt the passion of nationalism can understand and struggle with the conflict; only those whose passions are divided between nationalism and other commitments … can truly participate in the ongoing struggle for peace … The struggle of this insistent tradition of internationalist fantasy against the faithless … is not an unfortunate, irrational residue that needs to be gotten rid of … I propose to you this faith, this fantasy, as a precondition of international legal work … to have the conversion experience that will enable you to join us in this faith.[44]

The choice with these texts to cast international law as a priestly ordinance of the faithful is unmistakably evocative of the Christian tradition: the juxtaposition between those with and without faith, in the use of Orthodox Christian imagery (e.g., stained glass windows), in the equation of human rights and missionary evangelicalism. But, unlike the more overt apologetics of Harold Berman, this sensibility rejects any traditional denominational practice or belief. "It is probably that the world cannot live without religion," writes Allott:

> Obviously, I do not mean organized religion, ghastly churches and all the rest of it. Rather, I mean that human beings cannot lie without a transcendental or spiritual aspect to their lives … [S]ince the Holy Spirit must have brought you here, the reason must be to be born again. Or if you have been born again already, to be born again, again. Or if you have been born again already, to be born again, again! And so I will be praying as we go along that somebody may see the light at last …[45]

The differences, while real, belie a common pedigree. In a 2004 meeting in Munich, for instance, the philosopher Jürgen Habermas and then Prefect of the Roman Congregation for the Doctrine of the Faith, Joseph Ratzinger, met

---

44 Nathaniel Berman, "Legalizing Jerusalem or, Of Law, Fantasy, and Faith" 45 *Catholic University Law Review* 823, 834–835 (1995–1996).

45 "Review Essay Symposium: Allott's Eunomia and The Health of Nations Thinking Another World: This Cannot Be How the World Was Meant to Be" 16:2 *European Society of International Law* 255, 267 (2004).

to discuss the "dialectics of secularisation" from their respective corners, "reason" and "religion." Whatever disagreement might have been imagined, Ratzinger and Habermas strike out a strikingly similar set of initial propositions. First, global antagonisms can only be met through democratic modes of law that embrace human rights and reasoned deliberation:

> We have the formation of a global community in which the individual political, economic, and cultural powers become increasingly dependent on one another ... It is the specific task of politics to apply the criterion of the law to power, thereby structuring the use of power in a meaningful manner. It is not the law of the stronger, but the strength of the law that must hold sway. Power structured by law, and at the service of the law, is the antithesis of violence, which is a lawless power that opposes the law ... And as a sheer matter of fact, the guarantee of a shared collaboration in the elaboration of the law and in the just administration of power is the basic argument that speaks in favor of democracy as the most appropriate form of political order ... [I]n order to appeal to the reason we share in common and to seek the basis for a consensus about the ethical principles of law in a secular, pluralistic society [that allows us to keep] open our awareness of the totality and of the broader dimensions of the reality of human existence ... we ought perhaps to amplify the doctrine of human rights with a doctrine of human obligations and of human limitations ...[46]

Second, the path towards a politics of open deliberation is at once universal in scope and the particular province of a Western lineage that marries philosophy and Christian faith. "Political liberalism," announces Habermas in the opening to his discussion, is

> a Kantian republicanism ... [that] understands itself as a nonreligious and postmetaphysical justification of the normative bases of the democratic constitutional state. This theory is in the tradition of a rational law ... If we look back over history, that a common religious background and a common language, and above all the newly awakened national consciousness, helped create a highly abstract solidarity on the part of the citizens ... This is because the mutual co-penetration of Christianity

46 Joseph Ratzinger, "That Which Hold the World Together: The Pre-political Moral Foundations of a Free State" in Jürgen Habermas and Joseph Ratzinger, *The Dialectics of Secularisation: On Reason and Religion* 55, 57, 70–71 (Igatius Press 2005).

> and Greek metaphysics not only produced the intellectual form of theological dogmatics and a hellenization of Christianity (which was not in every sense a blessing). It also promoted the assimilation by philosophy of genuinely Christian ideas. This work of assimilation has left its mark in normative conceptual clusters with a heavy weight of meaning, such as responsibility, autonomy, and justification; or history and remembering, new beginning, innovation, and return; or emancipation and fulfillment; or expropriation, internalization and embodiment, individuality and fellowship. Philosophy has indeed transformed the original religious meaning of these terms, but without emptying them through a process of deflation and exhaustion ... [in particular] the translation of the concept of "man in the image of God" into that of the identical dignity of all men that deserves unconditional respect ... [that] goes beyond the borders of one particular religious fellowship and makes the substance of biblical concepts accessible to a general public that also includes those who have other faiths and those who have none.[47]

And third, Ratzinger and Habermas express a similar vision about the nature of the crisis facing the international legal order and the role of Christianity in meeting that challenge. For Ratzinger, the primary danger to a democratic rule of law comes from the pathologies of religious obscurantism and mechanistic rationality. "We have seen that there exist pathologies in religion that are extremely dangerous and that make it necessary to see the divine light of reason as a 'controlling organ,'" Ratzinger explains:

> However, we have also seen in the course of our reflections that there are also pathologies of reason ... a hubris ... that is no less dangerous ... Accordingly, I would speak of a necessary relatedness between reason and faith and between reason and religion, which are called to purify and help one another ... [Without] succumbing to a false Eurocentrism ... [t]here can be no doubt that the two main partners in this mutual relatedness are the Christian faith and Western secular rationality.[48]

Emphasizing the groundlessness of secular rationality to rejuvenate itself and provide normative limits to its own reasoning, Habermas identifies its exchange with Christian faith in almost identical terms:

---

47 See Jürgen Habermas, "Pre-Political Foundations of the Democratic Constitutional State?" in Habermas and Ratzinger, supra note 46, at 45.

48 Id. at 77–79.

> [W]hen reason reflects on its deepest foundations, it discovers that it owes its origin to something else. And it must acknowledge the fateful power of this origin, for otherwise it will lose its orientation to reason in the blind alley of a hybrid grasp of control over its own self … Philosophy, too, has been led to a self-reflection with regard to its own religious-metaphysical origins … [recognizing that an] abstract solidarity, mediated by the law, arises among citizens only when the principles of justice have penetrated more deeply into the complex of ethical orientations of a given culture … In the post-secular society, there is an increasing consensus that certain phases of the "modernization of the public consciousness" involve the assimilation and the reflexive transformation of both religious and secular mentalities …[49]

What these various strands of apology share is the feeling that Christianity is still an important companion to the future of global governance, providing a necessary ethical orientation to ground principles of justice and community. In the abstract, an appeal to any universalizing Christian tradition will come across for many as parochial, if not a rather open nod to Western imperialism.[50] And yet, we can see in the above correspondences, these appeals continually re-occur in even the most agnostic expressions of law and politics. Christian thought remains the a priori companion to a cosmopolitan rule of law.[51] This might help us explain the discomfort even more open-minded academics and policy makers often seem to feel toward Islamic head-scarves or other non-Western religious norms. And it casts suspicion on the formal, agnostic universality of the discipline.[52] Is it possible to think international law outside Christianity in the nostalgia of when Europeans dominated the earth?

49 Id. at 40.

50 "For natural law like any universal principles – Christianity, civilisation, human rights, the rule of law – is not only a means to show respect but to erase the identity of the other. The idea of a single societas humanae, however noble an aspiration, may be used as a platform, or a pretence, for projecting European mores over the whole world … The encounter with the other is thus also an encounter with ourselves …" Martti Koskenniemi, "The Lady Doth Protest Too Much: Kosovo and the Turn To Ethics in International Law" 65:2 *Modern Law Review* 159 (2002).

51 See Alberto Toscano, "Fanaticism: A Brief History of the Concept' *Eurozine* (December 2006), available at http://www.eurozine.com/articles/2006-12-07-toscano-en.html.

52 Even adopting a "hermeneutic of suspicion" – an aptitude to critical reasoning – is not a culturally neutral act. Non-Western institutional frameworks of authority may simply operate according to different rules of calculation and debate in coordinating legitimate authority. Just like wearing a tie is not simply dressing professionally, so too our disciplinary sensibilities and sophisticated erudition. See John D. Haskell, "The Religion/

3 Varieties of Post-Foundationalism

To this point, international lawyers share a feeling that some spiritual recourse is needed to stem the loss of Western meaning, whether that occurs through anarchy or bureaucracy. Among more liberal scholars, spiritual bricolage is preferred, whereby religion is emptied of any substantive content to instead be a procedural norm, an almost aesthetic ideal. In practice, however, this strategy of accommodation tends to circle back into the very obstacles that it originally proposed to circumnavigate. So long as principles remain sufficiently abstract, there will be minimal controversy. But the devil is in the details and between conflicting positions the law must decide allocation and outcomes. If the justification for a choice relies on some form of "good reason," it falls into exactly the problem we sought to avoid in the first place by turning to a spiritual grounding for the community. Reason alone was not sufficient, simply another abstract idealism or cynical maneuver shading some specific political agenda. But if not recourse to the objective rationality of a community or humanity, then what? A goodly Christian heritage, substantive or procedural, does not actually seem to offer a different scenario, and in legal scholarship tends to just mean trying to live up to a cosmopolitan ideal of empathy toward "the other," humility in the face of subjective constraints, attuned to contingency ... All very worthy traits until confronted with female genital mutilation, parental refusal that their child undergo a lifesaving surgery, and so forth. We are back right where we started, armed with a moralism now couched in a quasi-spiritual register. As Judith Butler summarizes:

> The fear ... is that what is named as universal is the parochial property of dominant culture, and that "universalizability" is indissociable from imperial expansion. The proceduralist view seeks to sidestep this problem by insisting that it makes no substantive claims about human nature, but its exclusive reliance on rationality to make its claim belies this very assertion ... universality has been used to extend certain colonialist and

---

Secularism Debate in Human Rights Literature: Constitutive Tensions Between Christian, Islamic, and Secular Perspectives" in Martti Koskenniemi, Mónica García-Salmones Rovira and Paolo Amorosa (eds), *International Law and Religion: Historical and Contemporary Perspectives* (Oxford University Press 2018) 135. More uncomfortable, within our domestic Western world, what if something similar goes for the tension between "liberal cosmopolitan elite" and post-truth populism? For an insightful study into the 20th century history of governance expertise in the United States, see James Smith, *The Idea Brokers: Think Tanks and the Rise of the New Policy Elite* (Free Press 1991). I turn to this question in the conclusion of our study.

> racist understandings of civilized "man," to exclude certain populations from the domain of the human, and to produce itself as a false and suspect category.[53]

The theoretical field surrounding political theology, however, also contains another tradition of argument – what we might broadly designate as "post-foundational." As with the varieties of apology for a Christian heritage in the previous section, post-foundationalism claims that the international legal order faces a political and existential state of emergency that may only be met by becoming (re)attuned to the spiritual character of political identity.[54] To situate this in religious terminology, we could say that this crisis is perhaps a loss of faith, but in addition to loss, a search for some new or rejuvenated spiritual fidelity. Yet, unlike the earlier arguments that lament the loss of any sure foundation or end up nostalgically chasing after some earlier religious conviction, the suspicion that there is no transcendental reference point to provide certainty to our personal or public life is now appropriated as cause for celebration – the very precondition of human emancipation and political awareness.[55] If we stand on a void, this emptiness is our freedom. In this view, a paradoxical proposition: on the one hand, socio-political order relies on a (hidden) transcendent reference/s, but on the other hand, this reference/s is neither immune from revision (e.g., invented rather than "discovered," contested rather than "fixed" or "natural") nor located "outside" society and politics (e.g., neither pre-political nor carrying any metaphysical properties). Let us turn our attention to two aspects of this orientation. First, the politico-theological character of this constitutive void that facilitates and resists any concrete existence. And second, two distinct strategies of engagement that have developed in response to the [un]grounding of international law – what we might call the orders of the "phallus" and the "not-All."

3.1 *The Constitutive [un]Grounding of International Law*

If the divine was no longer in the clouds, it remained a powerful motif in Western political thought. At times, it took the form of a metaphysical force manifesting itself in human affairs – for instance, with Adam Smith's Invisible Hand

---

53 Judith Butler, "Restaging the Universal" in Judith Butler, Ernesto Laclau, and Slavoj Žižek, *Contingency, Hegemony and Universality: Contemporary Dialogues on the Left* (Verso 2000) 15, 38.

54 See Hent de Vries, "Introduction: Before, Around, and Beyond the Theologico-Political" in de Vries and Sullivan, supra note 3 at 1.

55 Id.

or Hegelian Idealism.[56] In the 19th century, the ineffability of transcendence commonly took an explicitly geographic register as the colonial frontier, promising emancipation and rebirth.[57] As such, individuals could now more directly participate in this divine act of creation, "the endlessly reenacted moral event of writing human community into existence."[58]

This combination of a receding transcendence and humanity's participation in divinity became more pronounced in the aftermath of the first World War throughout Europe. Interwar intellectuals sought to undercut the cant of progress and the reliance on what were depicted as "traditional" modes of belief, whether towards civilization, nature or spirituality. On the one hand, this meant forgoing what was seen as the over-reliance on science/technology, which had not only failed to facilitate human sociability but actually escalated human suffering to mass industrial proportions.[59] On the other hand, the staid conventions, rituals, and beliefs that pacified past generations were now in hindsight ignorant hubris, absurdly comical if not their catastrophic

56 For an apologetic discussion around this theme, see Jacob Viner, *The Role of Providence in the Social Order: An Essay in Intellectual History* (originally printed 1972, Princeton University Press 1976). A common trope in Hegel and Smith – and themselves part of a long intellectual tradition to this day – is that the "public" or "universal" is within the "private" or "particular." See Akbar Rasulov, *Universality and the Ruses of the International Law Reason: A Tale of Two Scandals*, Lecture at the International University College of Turin Institute for Political Economy and Law Seminar Series (March 2011), available at https://www.youtube.com/watch?v=zToDR1jVqAU; John Haskell and Akbar Rasulov, "International Law and the Turn to Political Economy" 31:2 *Leiden Journal of International Law* 243 (2018). I will pick up on this theme again later in the text.

57 See Kerwin Lee Klein, *Frontiers of Historical Imagination: Narrating the European Conquest of Native America, 1890–1990* (University of California Press 1997) 176, 226. Of course, the frontier was not without its own contradictions and dangers. Weber, for instance, views the frontier as escaping European class structures – the very stuff of the New World promise from Old World cultured society – and for this very reason is capable of offering the possibility of a more equal and civil society. But following the frontier meant its eventual closure, and with it the future prospects of civilization's march toward greater democratic progress. See Will Wright, *The Wild West: The Mythical Cowboy and Social Theory* (Sage Publications 2001) 120–121.

58 Klein, supra note 57 at 77.

59 While the majority of academic disciplines, scientific communities, industries and politicians tend to view technology with tempered optimism, literature seems on the whole far more wary. A classic example of this, prescient for its time, that comes to my mind is the depiction of unexpected trench warfare that destroys society in Mark Twain's 1889 novel, *A Connecticut Yankee in King Arthur's Court*. See John Limon, *Writing After War: American War Fiction from Realism to Postmodernism* (Oxford University Press 1994) 50–52. Science fiction seems the genre par excellence for depicting technology as harbinger or representation of dystopia. For instance, see William Gibson, *Neuromancer* (Ace Books 1984); Neal Stephenson, *Snow Crash* (Bantam Books 1992).

consequences. If spirituality was to be found, it would be located in subjective intuition or non-Western culture. And even then, only ever as something forever incomplete, truth derived from appreciation of unending tensions, the impossible resolution of kairos and practice, of utopia and apology.[60] We can see versions of this across the cultural landscape of the time from art to law: in the Heideggerian idea of Ab-Grind as the intricate relation and reversibility of the ground and the abyss in a never-ending happening, in Joyce's quest for a universalizing synthetic formal gesture that allows for an infinite multiplicity of languages in its refusal of any culmination, in Bartok's musical aspirations to merge the extremes of high culture and primitive/peasant culture towards some authentic, uncontaminated echo of the sublime, in the jurisprudential theory of Redslob and other interwar jurists to marry the "nearly irreconcilable adversaries" of nationalist (primitive) passion and (civilized) legality.[61]

The constitutive void is loosely organized around the mainline account of Western disenchantment, with the twist that as intellectuals increasingly accepted God to be an unhelpful illusion, they found a compelling demand remained to preserve some religious analogy to understand the nature of political (if not personal) existence. In perhaps the most famous articulation of the continued importance of Christianity in understanding secular modernity, the Nazi jurist Carl Schmitt writes in 1922:

> All significant concepts of the modern theory of the state are secularized theological concepts not only because of their historical development – in

60 I will develop this theme throughout the text moving forward, as the logic of the "not-All," of the mystic stance, of post-foundational liberal cosmopolitanism.

61 For a discussion of modernism and its reflection in international law, see Nathaniel Berman, "Modernism, Nationalism, and the Rhetoric of Reconstruction" 4:2 *Yale Journal of Law and the Humanities* 351 (1992). Or finding its way into mathematics (via philosophy): "It is only when the mark disappears that its place appears, and therefore the mark as such … it attains its being only in its disappearance … the being of the mark, just like that of lack, 'exists' only in the in-between, incorporeal, ungraspable, or in the difference between the one and the other, in the movement, in the passage, and it is always either too early or to late … This process … itself [is] untotalizable … [a] multiplicity irreducible to a unity … We touch upon the impossible of the bi-univocal correspondence between the parts of U and the elements of U. The resource of multiplicity of the parts overflows the elementary multiplicity in which it is rooted … [Unlike] the unlimitation of Hegelian knowledge (absolute knowledge) [which] must include a principle of totality, the 'circle of circles' of its exhaustion … for us Cantorians, the notion that there is a whole of knowledge falls short of true unlimitation, which is the immanent movement of the excess over all conceived totality." Alain Badiou, *Theory of the Subject* (originally published 1982, Continuum 2009) 133, 218, 279 (in the first line of thought quoting from the psychoanalyst, Jacques-Alain Miller).

> which they were transferred from theology to the theory of the state, whereby, for example, the omnipotent God became the omnipotent lawgiver – but also because of their systematic structure, the recognition of which is necessary for a sociological consideration of these concepts … Only be being aware of this analogy can we appreciate the manner in which the philosophical ideas of the state developed in the last centuries … We have deservedly transferred the model of our division from theology to jurisprudence because the similarity of these two disciplines is astonishing.[62]

Of course, living in a world of secularized theological concepts implies a slight quaintness among those who continue to remain faithful to the presence of an omnipotent God of scripture.[63] Sincere religious adherents who accept some Fatherly presence or active divine intelligence outside of human history are seen, despite any public statements of acceptance, to have simply missed the memo.[64] But, at the same time, secularism without spirituality ostracizes the majority of the world's population (who are religious) and, as we have seen, faces the dilemma of providing a universalizing justification to authoritative claims. The constitutive void seems an attractive alternative for grounding the legitimacy of international law, offering meaning and direction in a world bereft of meta-narratives.[65]

This idea of the transcendent as an open horizon of withdrawal, however, is not a recent invention, but in fact a reoccurring Christian motif. We will

62 Schmitt, supra note 5 at 36, 37.

63 This comes in two varieties of global governance: the agnostic and the ecumenical, their differences more a matter of preference in tone than any substantive disagreement. Nor does either position exclude belonging to a denomination or creed, so long as one's faith is bracketed as personal and framed in ethical universalizing terms. See, for example, Richard Falk, *Religion and Humane Global Governance* (Palgrave Macmillan 2001). The choice of religion in this context is largely a matter of cultural background or individual choice rather than something actually debatable about the objective content of a decision. Something of intense devotion seems lost; this is not the faith of Abraham. As David Mamet puts it, "If you take the faith out of Religion, you have a wasted Sunday morning." David Mamet, *Writing in Restaurants* (Penguin 1987) 80. Perhaps more troubling, the whole affair suggests the rhetoric of subjective choice and consumer liberty – a thoroughly chastised faith to the dictates of market rationality. See William E. Connolly, *Capitalism and Christianity: American Style* (Duke University Press 2008).

64 For a classic derision of the faithful in legal academic literature, see Jerome Franck, *Law and the Modern Mind* (originally published 1936, Stevens & Sons 1949).

65 For a discussion about the character of this disavowal of meta-narratives and partisan stances among large sections of the intelligentsia, see Alain Badiou, *The Century* (originally published 2005, Polity Press 2007).

explore this in more detail further along, but take now for instance the figure of Jesus Christ mediated by the Apostle Paul. As intimated by his virgin birth, Jesus is God. "In the beginning was the Word, and the Word was with God, and the Word was God" (John 1:1). And yet, Jesus is also human, "the Word ... made flesh" (John 1:14). This paradoxical nature, the ability to raise the dead and also sweat tears of blood in anxiety over his crucifixion, provides an archetype of the relationship between the particular and universal: the essence of Jesus lies in exactly that space of resistance to collapsing into the fully human or the fully divine, an excess that is "God, but ...," and likewise, "human, but...."[66] In Pauline teaching, though there is little doubt that Paul saw Jesus as the literal Messiah to all humanity, the symbolic "empty" nature of Jesus is already prevalent in the call to the sinner, allowing for an infinite multiple to partake in messianic time and share in the spiritual aesthetic of becoming a new subject. "I have been crucified with Christ," writes Paul, "and it is no longer I who live, but Christ lives in me."[67] And yet, as history has demonstrated, Christ (as presence or ideal) living in us does not guarantee any necessary results, and like all other profound truths is a Janus-faced proposition. It is this indeterminacy that we now turn to explore.

3.2 *The Orders of the Phallus and the not-All*

In response to the recognition of an underlying groundlessness to any politico-legal regime, international lawyers within the post-foundational tradition have produced two contrasting arguments. In the first, what we may draw from psychoanalytical philosophy to name the "phallic" position, this ambiguity or void is filled by a sovereign who guarantees the maintenance of order but is ultimately beyond the rules of such order. In the original Freudian formula of the phallus, children (boy and girl) share the knowledge of only one genital (the penis) and the experience of castration: for the girl, in the belief that her mother lives with a severed penis, subsequently coming to idealize her father's intact fullness; for the boy, in suppressing (castrating) sexual desire for his mother in fear that his father will lop off his member as punishment. The penis becomes the unitary trait of identification establishing the father as the symbolic phallus, both the exception to castration and the particular site of obedience – what Lacan coins in the 1950s as "the All."[68] In religious

66 For a discussion of Jesus' relevance in this context, see Alain Badiou, *St. Paul: The Foundation of Universalism* (originally published 1997, Stanford University Press 2003).

67 *Galatians* 2:19–20 (New King James Version).

68 For a useful explanation of Lacan's thought and how it relates to psychoanalytic and philosophical literary traditions, see Lorenzo Chiesa, *Subjectivity and Otherness: A Philosophical Reading of Lacan* (MIT Press 2007).

terminology, therefore, we could equate the symbolic phallus with either the more conventional example of the Monotheistic God of the Old Testament, or more perversely, the figure of Jesus. In the first case, the Fatherly figure that often emerges in the Old Testament scriptures demands total devotion and obedience ("Thou shall have no other gods before me"), and establishes a rigid hierarchical legal structure to identify the "chosen" and mete out mortal punishment for any possible derogation from his absolute, undifferentiated rulership. In the second case, the depiction of Jesus in the Gospel account kills off the previous symbolic order (of the Jewish law and the Father) not to instigate a kinder face to authority as often depicted, but rather to enact an even more totalizing drive for authority. The public confession of faith demanded of each believer in the New Testament is alone not sufficient, faith must now be sincerely and completely internalized in the believer's heart.[69] It is not enough to obey, you must really love your master. He comes to you as servant or conduit, and yet solidifies a debt (the wages of sin) which is credited through his death and resurrection at the expense of an obligation, to love him and pray without ceasing in all things that you do.[70] In international legal discourse, the logic of the phallus is most often associated with the 19th and early 20th century Eurocentric patriarchal character of the colonial experience (e.g., civilization, logic), the fascistic/dictatorial regimes during the interwar period (especially expressed through the writings of Carl Schmitt), and more recently, in the competing master-narratives of communism and American-style globalization.[71] Let us explore this through Schmitt as he is perhaps most commonly vilified for this standpoint.

---

69 For a discussion engaging this general theme, see Kenneth Reinhard, "Toward a Political Theology of the Neighbor" in Slavoj Žižek, Eric L. Santner, and Kenneth Reinhard, *The Neighbour: Three Inquiries in Political Theology* (University of Chicago Press 2005) 11.

70 I will pick up on this theme later, but the basic formula of credit-debt-obligation derives out of a specific tradition of thinking about money. See Christine Desan, *Making Money: Coin, Currency, and the Coming of Capitalism* (Oxford University Press 2014); David Gerber, *Debt: The First 5,000 Years* (Melville House 2011); Randall L. Wray, *Modern Money Theory: A Primer on Macroeconomics for Sovereign Monetary Systems* (Palgrave Macmillan 2011). I am especially grateful to the communities around the Association for the Promotion of Political Economy and Law (APPEAL), the Institute for Global Law and Policy (IGLP), and Modern Money Theory (MMT) for countless conversations and time better understanding the history, regulation and theory of money. For a book just arriving that weaves together a study of aesthetics, money and religion, see Scott Ferguson, *Declarations of Dependence: Money, Aesthetics, and the Politics of Care* (University of Nebraska Press 2018).

71 The terminology moving forward makes use of psychoanalytic literary terms, such as the phallus and the "not-All," which are often quasi-gendered: the phallus often linked to "masculine" traits (e.g., aggression) and the not-All representing "feminine" attributes

In the "phallic" position, the (un)grounding of any historically limitless agent (e.g., God) or faculty of mind (e.g., reason) poses an imminent threat to the moral and material progress of the Western political order. In Schmitt's jurisprudence, this is due to a fundamental misunderstanding about two fundamental axioms of human existence (concerning sovereignty and community). Discarding the possibility of returning to a literal faith in the Christian scriptures, Schmitt never-the-less holds that these axioms can only be understood through the Genesis account of God's creation: first, an "extraordinary and fully arbitrary intervention of creation ex nihilo into the darkness of primal chaos" (e.g., the exception/miracle, sovereignty), and second, as a division or cut of this void into "stable oppositions of light and darkness" (e.g., friend-enemy).[72] To suppress the mystically produced nature of sovereignty and community, Schmitt argues, not only opens the door to the calamities of a global police state and wars of total annihilation, but obstructs the possibility of enabling political transparency and holding decision-makers morally responsible.

Concerning the conditions of sovereignty, the Genesis account instructs us that sovereign power is not based upon any contractual or discursive (democratic) or existing normative (legal) conditions, but is instead premised on the capacity to create something from (relative) nothingness. "[The] constitutive, specific element of a decision … cannot be anticipated … [and] is, from the

(e.g., listening). For a particularly eccentric example, see Thomas Baty, *International Law in Twilight* (Maruzen 1954) (his introduction drawing heavily upon his alter ego, Irene Clyde). There is something often troubling about how these positions are gendered, and more generally, I am personally rather not terribly interested with using psychoanalytic thought as an analytical toolkit. For an explanation of the limitations of psychoanalysis and offering an alternative systems-theory method, see Paul Watzlawick, Janet Beavin Bavelas, and Don Jackson, *Pragmatics of Human Communication: A Study of Interactional Patterns, Pathologies and Paradoxes* (W.W. Norton 1967). I work within these gendered terms in this text simply to try and address political theology in international legal scholarship on its own terms.

72 See Reinhard, supra note 69 at 14–15. "In the beginning God created the heaven and the earth. And the earth was without form, and void; and darkness was upon the face of the deep. And the Spirit of God moved upon the face of the waters. And God said, Let there be light; and there was light … and God divided the light from the darkness." *Genesis* 1:1–4 (King James Version). Often passed over, there is a break between the first and second sentence of Genesis: heaven and earth are created, and then we learn that the earth is "without form, and void" and covered in water, "the deep." Water is a symbol of judgment (e.g., Noah's flood) and I would follow those Biblical scholars that suggest this implies a previous creation that was judged. Scripture teaches us that creation poses itself as created out of nothing, but is always actually working in the remnants of some existing conditions.

perspective of the content of the underlying norm, new and alien ... created out of nothingness."[73] If the precondition of existence is nothingness, then the divine spark of life depends on a moment of rupture that is solely dependent on a decision, a will to power, a founding call or naming, which operates like kairos to arise completely unexpected, like "a thief in the night"[74] – or what Schmitt describes in a theistic/theological register as "the miracle," or more commonly referenced by international lawyers, the "exception."[75] Here, the sovereign in none other than the (divine) agent capable of standing in and filling the void, the guarantor of the politico-moral order, dictatorial in the capacity to simultaneously declare the exception (miraculous in being previously impossible and beyond reason) and enforce its decision (the incarnation of its word as its own justification).[76] Sovereignty, in Schmitt's words, is a

---

73 Schmitt, supra note 5 at 6, 66.

74 There are a number of verses in the New Testament that speak to the theme of the "thief in the night." The most ominous and closest to our reading in *Revelation* 16:15 (King James Version): "Behold, I come as a thief. Blessed is he that watcheth and keepeth his garments, lest he walk naked, and they see his shame."

75 The *Oxford Dictionary* defines exception as a "[b]reach of a covenant, intercourse, or the peace ... a breach of harmony or friendly relations between two persons or parties ... a breach of continuity; interruption ... the act of breaking out into arms ... a break in a surface or substance, such as the skin, flesh, etc ... a break in the surface of the earth, etc.; a ravine, chasm, gorge, rift ... the act of breaking or bursting; the fact of being broken or burst ..." The word 'miracle' is explained as "[a]n extraordinary and welcome event that is not explicable by natural or scientific laws and is therefore attributed to a divine agency ... a remarkable event or development that brings very welcome consequences ... an exceptional product or achievement, or an outstanding example of something." Exception and miracle, in our English vernacular, denote very different occurrences: exception signaling a disruptive rupture, whereas miracle suggesting a positive development, and whereas the exception does not necessarily imply a given actor, miracles seem to require a primary agent. There is a significant difference in terminology between the popular vernacular and political theology scholarship.

76 See Schmitt, supra note 5 at 66. This act of "declaring" or "naming" within a system runs throughout his thinking, usually linked to his ties with fascism. This seems to me an overly narrow reading of Schmitt, which ignores his antipathy to market rationality and the long tradition of economic thought spanning left and right orientations that situates human emancipation in the expansion of distribution and/or production. For Schmitt, distribution and production must always be located within historically discrete contexts, which is organised in the wake of an original appropriation that determines the core cultural, economic and political rules of a given time and place. The logic of appropriation, not that of distribution or production, is determining in the last instance. It names, or calls, or interpolates people as subjects. Here Schmitt looks not all that different from many Marxist theorists. See Carl Schmitt, "Appropriation/Distribution/Production: Toward a Proper Formulation of Basic Questions of any Social and Economic Order" 95 *Telos* 52 (1993); Schmitt, supra note 33 at 336.

"borderline" concept, standing outside the legal order yet constituting its internal measure, the corruption and infallibility of a given politico-legal regime (e.g., the absolute State, the Leviathan), what we previously identified with the role of the symbolic phallus.[77] The legal order, therefore, far from standing outside of power looking in, is always itself the concrete realization of discrete political decisions behind which stands a dictatorial whim to ensure the internal cohesion (obedience) of its constituency.

The tendency to view Schmitt's writings as a cynical transfer of religious themes to support fascistic politics undercuts the fact that Schmitt here is operating within an almost completely (liberal) Christian tradition. In the first place, the animosity towards the "rule of law" as "of this world" and an obstacle to an individual's authenticity or righteousness is a familiar trope in Christian theology. In medieval times, the politico-theological doctrinal debates between those who believed God bound by the laws of creation (whether or not created by God) and others who emphasized the ability of God to stand outside and violate the rules of creation already intimates some struggle over how to conceptualize political power in relation to law.[78] Or in the late modern era in Western Europe, between deistic and naturalist Christians who saw an almost mechanical creation, versus existential Christians, such as Kierkegaard, who emphasized the miraculous core of faith that defied any reason or experience.[79] And throughout the 20th century, the aversion to the technological routinization of humanity as an animal or machine, of the natural sciences' denial of religion's affirmation in the inborn human dignity that defies empirical proof.[80]

---

77 See Schmitt, supra note 5 at 55.

78 There is a rich literature on the medieval era writ large in relation to governance. For just a few of many directions, see Gordon Leff, *Heresy in the Later Middle Ages: The Relation of Heterodoxy to Dissent: 1250–1450*, 2 vols. (Manchester University Press 1967); James Muldoon, *Popes, Lawyers and Infidels: The Church and the Non-Christian World, 1250–1500* (University of Pennsylvania Press 1979); Brian Tierney, *The Idea of Natural Rights: Studies of Natural Rights, Natural Law and Church Law, 1150–1625* (Scholars Press 1997).

79 "The exception explains the general and itself. And if one wants to study the general correctly, one only needs to look around for a true exception. It reveals everything more clearly than does the general. Endless talk about the general becomes boring; there are exceptions. If they cannot be explained, then the general also cannot be explained. The difficulty is usually not noticed because the general is not thought about with passion but with a comfortable superficiality. The exception, on the other hand, thinks the general with intense passion." Soren Kierkegaard, *Repetition* (originally published 1843, Princeton University Press 1983) 227. For an interesting discussion around this engagement between Kierkegaard and Schmitt, see Jacob Taubes, *To Carl Schmitt: Letters and Reflections* (Cambridge University Press 2013) 40.

80 The antipathy to bureaucracy is a favourite villain of post mid-20th century Western culture: in Pink Floyd's *Another Brick in the Wall*, in Terry Gilliam's cinematic masterpiece

In the second place, the concept of the "exception" (a rupture from an existing order that founds a new creation) is also an explicit motif reoccurring throughout the Christian scriptures: in the Genesis account (from the darkness and void of an old earth, covered in water), in the Revelation promise of a new earth (from the Lake of Fire, which consumes the evil of this age), and with the death and resurrection of Jesus. In Pauline Christianity, the "exception" of Jesus' resurrection fulfils and undermines the Judaic law, symbolized in the Gospels by the tearing of the veil separating the Holy of Holies (that housed the divinity of God) from the pedestrian space of the Jewish temple, collapsing the formal rule of the law that mediated between God and humanity in favour of a new confessional aesthetic. The freedom from one law, in other words, does not release the Christian believer into uncharted emancipation, but instead demands a new perhaps even weightier burden. As we already have seen in the New Testament, one can no longer merely follow the law, one must internalize the spirit of the law, which in turn challenges the faithful to develop techniques to test and determine the success of their self-discipline and commitment – what we might be able to see as the early precursors to the modern fetish of signifiers that Schmitt advances, such as "transparency," "individual responsibility," and "moral agency" (what Foucault would more ominously coin as "governmentality").[81] For Schmitt, the duty of the believer

Brazil, in the CIA funded Cold War era paintings of Jackson Pollock, and throughout Herbert Marcuse's 1964 text *One Dimensional Man*. If we pull back to earlier decades, however, bureaucracy loses its oppressive character. Intellectuals in the 19th century tended to wax optimistic about expanding organizational infrastructure and institutional processes. Even in Kafka, there is an eroticism to bureaucracy's violence, just as Chaplain may condemn the assembly line but his alternative cannot imagine itself beyond a wholly nostalgic pastoral-esc fantasy. Contemporary legal thought is undecided about bureaucracy: on the one hand, authors call for normative orders requiring sweeping bureaucratic infrastructures to address all sort of dangers and problems in global governance, but on the other hand, will often lament bureaucratic blindness to human need and freedom. Bureaucracy is the backbone of working class professionalization and social power, and all-too-often its critics are trapped within Cold War imaginations or conflate bureaucracy and process with an assessment/auditing culture, a very different beast of the post 1960s. For discussions around some of these themes, see David Graeber, *The Utopia of Rules: On Technology, Stupidity and the Secret Joys of Bureaucracy* (First Melville House 2015); Michael Power, *The Audit Society: Rituals of Verification* (Oxford University Press 1997).

81 See Michel Foucault, *The Birth of Biopolitics: Lectures at the College de France 1978–1979* (originally published 2004, Palgrave Macmillan 2008). The general observation here, is that discipline takes different forms, and sometimes the more intrusive the discipline the more it may appear, by contrast, less severe. Once upon a time, we were called to work and worship by the ringing of the church bells, just as when we are children there is a buzzer at school to announce when class is about to begin. You hear the bell, and you are to scurry obediently to your place. A clear hierarchy of authority is at play in

is to submit to the incarnation of the Word made flesh (e.g., the Führer) in an outward and inward act of constant fidelity, to "pray without ceasing" in "fear and trembling." Thus, against the softer liberal versions of Jesus that are so often juxtaposed against a vengeful, bronze-age deity, Schmitt points us to the realization that the Jesus of the Christian scriptures stands as the ultimate representation of the charismatic sovereign, who declares a new commandment into existence (e.g., "love your enemies"), which is "not merely new, but antinomian" in complete violation of the preexisting legal code (e.g., "judge thine enemy"), what the philosopher Kenneth Reinhard explains is not only an "exercise of the sovereign prerogative of exception [to suspend a law that did not previously exist], but an act of politico-theological creation ex nihilo, truly a polemical miracle,"[82] and which demands a full and sincere interiorization of the sovereign will (e.g., not only over the body, but now also the mind).[83] If Schmitt's logic is the stuff of fascism, it (like liberalism) draws deep from the well of Christianity.

This notion of a rupture from a previous fabric, of a decision that tears through a prior state of affairs, leads us now beyond the division between law and lawlessness and the enactment of sovereignty, to the second axiom of the politico-theological: the bringing together of a multitude of dispersed individual wills to form a body politic, the community. Drawing upon the model of the

---

such institutions: the church bell clangs from above us by officials higher in the chain of authority, the student tardy to class may be sent to the office for disciplinary procedures, robbed of playtime with after-school detention and notice sent home to parents. The end of the age of church bells and school buzzers seems to inaugurate a certain degree of personal autonomy and freedom. Just think of Jules Verne's *Around the World in 80 Days* – among other things, a celebration of the pocket watch, a catechism for the modern man, its protagonist possessing time and by extension able to control and manipulate its confines around his ingenuity. One no longer is called by time; quite the opposite, one now sets their own calendar, on their terms. The same is true once we leave school and head to university, or into more privileged positions of the workforce. We are adults who can make our own decisions; we set our own alarm clocks. But is this freedom or the internalization of discipline, of becoming one's own warden, of internalizing the costs of enforcement? Self-determination perhaps, but a determination of the self by the self to enslavement – a style of masochism. See Jacques Le Goff, *Time, Work, and Culture in the Middle Ages* (University of Chicago Press 1980).

82 Reinhard, supra note 69 at 18.

83 The bar for the believer's sincerity is set high. "Not every one that saith unto me, Lord, Lord, shall enter into the kingdom of heaven; but he that doeth the will of my Father which is in heaven. Many will say to me in that day, Lord, Lord, have we not prophesied in thy name? and in thy name have cast out devils? and in thy name done many wonderful works? And then will I profess unto them, I never knew you: depart from me, ye that work iniquity." *Matthew* 7:21–23 (King James Version). The Calvinist insecurity over salvation is understandable.

Catholic Church, Schmitt seeks to institutionalize a clear distinction between the faithful and the damned in this life and frame this opposition in starkly public terms. In the Catholic context, the church claims absolute power in the ecclesiastic hierarchy to rule as spiritual and intellectual guide over all human activity. Schmitt posits this same operation necessary in political life:

> The distinction of friend and enemy denotes the utmost degree of intensity of a union or separation, of an association or dissociation … The political enemy need not be morally evil or aesthetically ugly; he need not appear as an economic competitor, and it may even be advantageous to engage with him in business transactions. But he is, nevertheless, the other, the stranger; and it is sufficient for his nature that he is, in a specifically intense way, existentially something different and alien, so that in the extreme case conflicts with him are possible … [who in] the extreme case of conflict … must be repulsed or fought in order to preserve one's own form of existence.[84]

What Schmitt brings to light here in the founding of each new community is the inescapability of some moment of pure antagonism, the occurrence of friend ("we") and enemy ("them") that suggests violent sacrifice. This is again a thoroughly Christian understanding of human nature and politics, and which has found its way into our own era, through Schmitt and Strauss, living today within realist doctrines in international relations. In a sinful world beyond redemption, where humanity stands always on the precipice of falling into a Hobbesian state of nature bereft of God, internal stability and peace may only be achieved through discrete political units organized under some stern judge attuned to the dangers of humanity's sin nature. If humanity is a brotherhood, it is the brotherhood of Cain and Abel and at their peril political leaders forget the tragic hubris of the builders of Babel to unite all people in one language and cause.[85] Since humanity is inherently political, and the political is ineradicably antagonistic, the solution for Schmitt is to avoid deluding oneself (as he believed of liberal democratic jurists) that humanity carries any natural sociability that can be brought out through deliberative values, and to instead openly project our inbred violence vertically (the enforcement of the sovereign prerogative) and horizontally (the "battling totality" united by a common foe).

---

84 Schmitt, supra note 5 at 27.

85 See Arthur A. Leff, "Unspeakable Ethics, Unnatural Law" 6 *Duke Law Journal* 1229, 1249 (1979).

Especially in relation to its external foe, this pure antagonism that founds the political community therefore carries an explicit spatial character:

> In the beginning was the fence. Fence, enclosure, and border are deeply interwoven in the world formed by men, determining its concepts ... Every new age and every new epoch in the coexistence of peoples, empires, and countries, of rules and power formations of every sort, is founded on new spatial divisions, new enclosures and new spatial orders of the earth ... The enclosure gave birth to the shrine by removing it from the ordinary, placing it under its own laws, and entrusting it to the divine. The enclosing ring ... is a primeval form of ritual, legal and political cohabitation ... law and peace originally rested on enclosures in a spatial sense. In particular, it was not the abolition of war, but rather its bracketing that has been the great core problem of every legal order ... A meridian decides the truth.[86]

In his 1950 publication, *The Nomos of the Earth in the International Law of the Jus Publicum Europaeum*, Schmitt specifically places the origins of this spatial character of the "history of peoples" in the Old Testament books of *Numbers* and *Joshua* (the "classic example"), which recount the appropriation of the promised land of Canaan by the tribes of Israel. Schmitt does not go into the details of the Biblical story, but links it to the emergence and success of the medieval Catholic Church, and later, Western Europe during the Age of Discovery: the Church organized around the "dangerous foe" of Islam, Western Europe bracketing war to achieve formal internal peace by projecting its national rivalries to the "free space" of the colonial outskirts.[87] The danger, in Schmitt's mind, is that the internalization of anti-colonial rhetoric within the Western European order, the rise of the United States as the sole military superpower, and the expansion of a worldwide capitalist-oriented economic framework of governance have resulted in the disappearance of any further possibility of territorial escape or clearly defined enemy. Without an external antagonism defined around spatial lines, the international order faces the inevitable psychosis of the paranoid global police state haunted by almost-invisible threats – what Jacques Derrida, echoing Schmitt, describes as

> ... an unheard-of violence, the evil of a malice knowing neither measure nor ground, an unleashing incommensurable in its unprecedented – therefore

86 See Schmitt, supra note 33 at 74, 95.

87 Id.

> monstrous – forms; a violence in the face of which what is called hostility, war, conflict, enmity, cruelty, even hatred, would regain reassuring and ultimately appeasing contours because they would be identifiable.[88]

In our times, Schmitt's fears seem especially realized by the policies in the United States and Western Europe institutionalizing the war on terror: the hostility toward minarets in Switzerland, banning headscarves in France, unchecked electronic surveillance of domestic everyday life, news outlets relating a civilization struggle between the "free" world and quasi-invisible terrorist cells. "Our values are worth struggling for [and] … represent humanity's progress throughout the ages and at each point we have had to fight for them and defend them," argued Tony Blair in a series of 2006–07 speeches, echoing this new nomo-less global order. "As a new age beckons, it is time to fight for them again … Terrorism destroys progress. Terrorism can't be defeated by military means alone. But it can't be defeated without it."[89] If this delinking of territory and authority in the name of some abstract "humanity" is the realization of Schmitt's anxiety however, it maintains his logic of an "us" from the "enemies of freedom." In other words, the terrorists function perhaps most tellingly as a metaphorical embodiment of the danger to the conceptual and material breakdown of a formalized meridian between neutrality and total war (that previously existed between European states and non-European "free land"). Without an external enemy on terrestrial grounds, conflicts proliferate in atomized, tribal conflicts within the previously orderly borders of nation states, requiring new oppressive measures by paranoid governments to halt, if possible, the dissolution of society itself. In a distinctly Calvinist sentiment, the chosen are faced now with a radical insecurity about their future.

The difficulty for many international lawyers – who take seriously the horrors of the colonial experience and fascism – is there seems no readily ascertainable road forward once we accept an utterly lawless abyss underlying any normative order, regardless of how benevolent a regime may appear or how ruthless an external threat presents itself at first glance. If we oppose empire, for example, then it is near impossible to accept (even on good faith) the United States' claim to stand in the void as the unconditional sovereign, the global policeman, charged with upholding some world constitution.[90] How-

88 Jacques Derrida, *The Politics of Friendship* (originally published 1994, Verso 2005) 83.

89 Quoted and discussed in Gray, supra note 6 at 74–106.

90 There is a significant literature in the legal academy built on linking contemporary American governance to the legacies of colonialism and imperialism. For example, see Antony Anghie, *Imperialism, Sovereignty and the Making of International Law* (Cambridge University Press 2004); China Miéville, *Between Equal Rights: A Marxist Theory of International*

ever, when we take a more cynical response to the universal rights claims deployed to justify the United States' unilateralism (or other political actors doing the same), we are left offering some alternative legal vocabulary to check political ambition (e.g., cosmopolitan federalism, human rights) that is also forced to ultimately acknowledge the need for some interpretative executive decision that privileges a particular agenda and actor(s), ironically re-enacting the very political fiat we sought to avoid. A common response in this situation is to find coherence in the processes and sensibility of the profession – the community that makes up the "rule of law." But this seems again unsatisfying. What if members within this community disagree (e.g., over context, interpretation, sources)? What if a perfectly salient legal position is countered by an equally justifiable counter-argument in law? At this point, advocates tend to suggest that the more reasonable direction will manifest itself over time, so long as its practitioners remain true to their calling of "rightly dividing" the word. A faith in reason, or perhaps something altogether more metaphysical, the logic behind the story of Noah's Ark and Pascal's wager, or its movie equivalent, *Field of Dreams*: if you merely continue practicing your work in good conscience, the rest will take care of itself. Build the ark, the animals will come; maintain your ritualized worship, salvation is nigh; flatten your corn fields into a baseball field, the players and audience will arrive. But looking to the internal community of the law was offered initially as a response to the limits of reason. We have come full circle. Why should we trust this reason with all its blind spots, contradictions, gaps, and questionable neutrality? In danger of falling back on a discretionary political choice, therefore, the only option remaining seems to be to denounce the entire international legal framework itself as mere rhetorical gesture, either the cynical manipulation of powerful political actors or the fantastic daydreams of activists far removed from the daily affairs of real decision-making. To see international law simply as rhetoric, however, again circles us back to the necessity of offering some new vision, a (revolutionary) partisan stand that re-enacts some high stakes friend-enemy distinction, which in turn throws the original criticism of international law as "too political" back in our face. This difficulty is compounded by the fact that the 20th century projects of collective action (e.g., communist and third world revolutions) failed to establish social institutions free from the "taint of dependence and domination."[91] We appear doomed to ultimately submit to the undemocratic and antagonist nature of the political, inescapably forced to choose an apologetic demeanour

Law (Brill 2005); Akbar Rasulov, "Writing about empire: remarks on the logic of a discourse" 23:2 *Leiden Journal of International Law* 449 (2010).

91 Roberto Mangabeira Unger, *Social Theory: Its situation and its task* (Verso 2004) 1.

that borders on a disheartening conservative apathy, or alternatively to choose romantically – if not arbitrarily – from equally ungrounded political assessments over what constitutes legitimate and illegitimate forms of violence and who carries the exceptional capacity of enforcement. Within the logic of the phallic order, therefore, international lawyers are forced into the unsavoury task of willful self-duplicity: on the one hand, recognizing the radical yet necessary contingency of any political subject or social stability, and on the other hand, suppressing this knowledge of any authority's incomplete and transient nature in order to justify authority. And, all so often, our talk and writing just running the wheel of transcendental nonsense.[92]

If the phallocentric logic of castration exists in a state of compulsive anxiety seeking to locate some symbol that can routinize all erogenous zones (e.g., particular political desires) into a unified global field (e.g., the dictator, the party, the state), the "not-All" position holds that we are always already castrated and that the constitutive emptiness that grounds political identity (e.g., the void) undercuts any teleological aspiration before it is even declared. This stance draws out a double pretension here in the assertion of the symbolic phallus to be the "All." First, the very identity of the phallus depends on our ability to juxtapose it against something that it is not (hence eviscerating its totalizing aspirations). And second, since castration (the central fear of the phallic order) is in fact the very pre-condition of socio-political existence (as we are always already castrated), it is the supposed rationality and real politic of the phallus that is in fact hysterically delusional – why fear what is inevitably already the case and inescapable to avoid?

For the cosmopolitan enthusiast, this is cause for celebration. The de-centring of the universal no longer signals anarchy and chaos to international legal order, but is instead poised to re-invigorate the discipline's relevance in world affairs, widening the scope of engagement and inclusion to previously marginalized groups. To put this in economic terms, the not-All logic opens the marketplace of (ethical/political/legal) principles to new participants, increasing the wealth of established agents (e.g., European "high society"), transforming potential outlaws into stakeholders (e.g., formerly colonized classes), and cycling out dated wares in favour of new products (or at least, to extend our metaphor, repackaging them). The value of this logic is that it promises reform

92 I find Pierre Schlag particularly useful exploring these problems; for instance, see Pierre Schlag, *The Enchantment of Reason* (Duke University Press 1998). General attention to this problem, however, reoccurs throughout theoretical work in international law; for example, see Jean d'Aspremont, *International Law as a Belief System* (Cambridge University Press 2018).

without revolution, to make the world a more entertaining and lovely place through non-violent competition, to preserve and broadly distribute the best characteristics of capitalist modernity without cost. If the phallic order is constituted on fantasy, there is no reason that we cannot imagine the world in radically different terms. We are no longer condemned to an empirical, closed history or the traditional rituals of the dead. The current reality and the future is instead predicated on human imagination and potent agency. The role of the academic and policy maker is invested with a divine power, much like the priest during the act of transubstantiation, to the extent that it is no longer the purpose simply to study and interpret the natural order, but now to participate in the act of creating order from the void. As such, the logic recalibrates politico-legal debates to a politico-theological orientation that emphasizes ethical creativity, tolerant anti-imperialism, and mystic ineffability.

In the phallic position, ethical assessment only takes place if actors openly accept the hierarchic and arbitrary (and violent) nature of political life. The void in the phallic imagination is whatever lurks on the margins and beneath the political order that might obscure the legitimacy of absolute sovereignty (either disguising or fragmenting the "katechon"); in psychoanalytical terms, the source of castration anxiety. The logic of the not-All, however, proposes to circumvent this anxiety by accepting that being itself is constituted on an incompleteness. There is no unified corporeality, only "an infinite series of possible encounters, one without limit and without totalization, a field without the stability of margins."[93] The focus here is on the space between relationships, which serves as the very condition for human creativity and ethical judgment:

> Only if I experience the absolute as an utterly empty place can I project into contingent courses of action a moral depth ... the postmodern experience of the radical contingency of any particular content claiming to be morally valid is the very condition for the ethical over investment that makes possible a higher consciousness ... Serious moral engagement requires a radical separation between moral consciousness and its contents so that no content can have any a priori claim to be the exclusive beneficiary of the engagement ...[94]

Here, ethical behaviour is equated with the recognition of the ultimate contingency to any a priori truth and foregrounds the necessity to act in the face of uncertainty, taking responsibility for the consequences of our

93 Reinhard, Santner and Žižek, supra note 69 at 6.

94 Ernesto Laclau, "On the Names of God" in De Vries and Sullivan, supra note 3 at 137, 147.

decisions – what the existential Christian theology of Kierkegaard discussed as the "aporia" of responsibility. The responsible agent, deprived of precedent's comfort and aware of finitude, is forced into a leap of faith, which reveals a political and religious truth: that human freedom and morality are premised on a "lack" (of certainty, of totality). The phallic miracle that establishes the possibility of morality by forcefully suppressing its constitutive lack(s) is now re-appropriated by the not-All argument within international legal theory to serve as the basis for a formalized ethical sensitivity to marginalized actors and the consequences of political decisions:

> [T]he turn to ethics has also revealed a vulnerable spot ... There is no neutral terrain ... If law is inevitably always also about the subjective and the emotional, about faith and commitment, then nothing prevents re-imagining international law as commitment to resistance and transgression. Having learned its lessons, formalism might then re-enter the world assured that whatever struggles it will have to weigh, the inner anxiety of the Prince is less a problem to resolve than an objective to achieve ...[95]

Drawing language from Spivak, Australian legal theorist Anne Orford makes a similar argument, that the deconstruction of the ground or centre of international law is the precondition of the profession's capacity to experience the realization of justice and the hope of renewal:

> Here lies the possibility for remaking the law in the image of justice ... [We] can't avoid acts of exclusion ... [and the] drawing of boundaries ... [T]he end will be inconclusive ... [and we must not] forget the productive unease that what we do with the utmost care is judged in the margins ... [upon] the lack of firm ground.[96]

This attenuation to the constitutive emptiness and margins of being as the specific terrain of the "female space" is not only cause for ethical/creative joy, but also the last guard against the brutal hegemonic excesses of culture (e.g., Eurocentricity, patriarchy) and politics (e.g., colonialism, fascism, imperialism).[97] The female space ransacks the rigid universality of the phallic imagination

---

95 Koskenniemi, supra note 50 at 175.

96 Anne Orford, *Reading Humanitarian Intervention: Human Rights and the Use of Force in International Law* (Cambridge University Press 2003) 70–71.

97 As Alice Jardine suggests, "[T]he space outside of the conscious subject has always connoted the feminine in the history of Western thought – and any movement into alterity is a movement into that female space." Alice Jardine, "Gynesis" 12 *Diacritics* 54, 59–60 (1982).

that would circumscribe diversity under a particular set of hierarchically prescribed norms, unveiling that universality is actually the abstract designation of a dynamic exchange of infinite diversities and does not require forceful "imperialist" measures. Analogizing this open-ended process to the political sphere, Judith Butler explains:

> The claim to universality always takes place in a given syntax, through a certain set of cultural conventions in a recognizable venue ... But what orchestrates what will and will not become recognizable as a claim?... [T]here is no cultural consensus on an international level about what ought and ought not to be a claim to universality, how may make it, and what form it ought to take. Thus, for the claim to work, for it to compel consensus, and for the claim, performatively, to enact the very universality it enunciates, it must undergo a set of translations into the various rhetorical and cultural contexts in which the meaning and force of universal claims are made. Significantly, this means that no assertion of universality takes place apart from a cultural norm, and, given the array of contesting norms that constitute the international field, no assertion can be made without at once requiring a cultural translation ... without translation, the only way the assertion of universality can cross a border is through a colonial and expansionist logic.[98]

The attraction of this approach is that it reconciles the phallic understanding that political identity and legitimate action is always an antagonistic encounter of particular interests with the modern intellectual predisposition to anti-dogmatism (not to be confused with formalism) and taking stands against partisan power politics. Yes, the international political order is unstable, but instability is the very condition for dynamic exchange, and this open dynamism suggests both its continued newness/vitality and sensitivity/sincerity. For philosophers within the not-All or "feminine" position, such as Ernesto Laclau, cosmopolitan democracy is the concrete political expression of this anti-phallic openness, the nearest equation to the perennial experience or truth of the fragmented (e.g., antagonistic) and ungrounded nature of being:

> [A] system of oppression (that is of closure) can be combated in two different ways – either an operation of inversion which performs a new closure [the phallic logic], or by negating in that system its universal dimension the principle of closure as such. It is one thing to say that the

98 Butler, supra note 53 at 34–35.

> universalistic values of the west are the preserve of its traditional dominant groups; it is very different to assert that the historical link between the two is a contingent and unacceptable fact which can be modified through political and social struggles … to the demands of large sections of the population – minorities, ethnic groups and so on – who traditionally had been excluded from it … The unresolvable tension between universalism and particularism opens the way to a movement away from Western Eurocentrism … [whereby the] universal does not have a concrete content of its own (which would close it on itself), but is an always receding horizon resulting from the expansion of an indefinite chain of equivalent demands … This paradox cannot be solved, but … its non-solution is the very precondition of democracy … If democracy is possible, it is because the universal has no necessary body and no necessary content; different groups, instead, compete between themselves to temporarily give to their particularisms a function of universal representation.[99]

This philosophical pedigree of argument has become a fixture in international legal theory over the last decade. In his magisterial reflective study of the profession, *The Gentle Civilizer of Nations*, Koskenniemi channels the not-All position advanced by Laclau to conclude:

> To rid [international legal cosmopolitanism] of suspicion, [we] must remain open for other voices, other expressions of "lack" (or justice) that, when given standing under it, redefine the scope of its universality … [I]t has no essence, and techniques are constantly redefined in the context of political struggle what the particular lacks cannot be decided once and for all … Thus every decision process with an aspiration to inclusiveness must constantly negotiate its own boundaries as it is challenged by new claims or surrounded by new silences. Yet because it is unachieved, it can sustain (radical) democracy and political progress, and resist accepting as universal the claims it has done most to recognize in the past … a practice of decision making that persists … through which the aspirations of self-determining communities remain alive – even as (or perhaps precisely because) the universal they embody remains only a horizon … It represents the possibility of the universal (as Kant knew) but it does

---

99 Ernesto Laclau, *Emancipation(s)* (Verso 1996) 33–35.

this by remaining "empty," a negative instead of a positive claim, and thus avoids the danger of imperialism.[100]

Unlike the phallic "miracle" that looks for a charismatic hero (e.g., Schmitt's dictator) willing to step into the void and declare a one-to-one relationship with the universal (e.g., to embody the Lacanian Real), we should see here – in a religious context – that the ideological function of the not-All "belongs exclusively to the field of mystical experience" under the aegis of a messianic hope that calls upon the initiate to maintain the openness of the void – in a Heideggerian vein, to act as "guardians of the Open" against the tempting perditions to name "Who is the Cause of All Things."[101] Let us trace this eschatological hope and the role of the mystic through Christian theology to contemporary political philosophy and international legal theories in order to better understand the politico-theological stakes of this post-foundational orientation.

The eschatological hope focuses on a promise that historical time will culminate in some messianic fulfilment that has itself already been inaugurated in human history. In the scriptures, for instance, the Pentateuch narrative recounts the relationship between God and the Jewish people dating from their escape of slavery in Egypt to their entrance into the land of Canaan. This is a period of tribulation and testing as the price of being God's chosen people, with failure often occasioning draconian punishment (e.g., the earth swallowing up entire clans, the tribes cursed with plagues and famines). It is a cruel world, the presence of God like the promise of Canaan – always seemingly far-off (e.g., Moses is allowed to look but not touch the promised land). Between a cruel world and a distant God, armed with only the law and intimations of something beyond their finite conditions, the exodus is an account of the Jewish people's struggle to maintain fidelity to their God and the organizing vision of their politico-religious identity in the face of uncertainty and despair.[102] Against any proof, they are to remember the miracle of their escape through the Red Sea and the giving of the law at Mt. Sinai, of manna drifting down from heaven and the pillar of fire that guided their wanderings. These past events counsel against present despair to a future promise, despite any evidence to the contrary. In other words, the messianic event (whether that is the messiah or the promised land or a new Jerusalem) occurs as a radical disjunction

100 Martti Koskenniemi, *The Gentle Civilizer of Nations: The Rise and Fall of International Law, 1870–1960* (Cambridge University Press 2004) 504–507.

101 See Laclau, supra note 94 at 139.

102 I have taken this tension "between a cruel world and a distant God" from the work of Reut Paz, albeit used in a different context to look at the legacy of 20th century Jewish international jurists. See Paz, supra note 15.

with(in) the present, both in this world and belonging already to a coming age, that interrupts the common sense telos of the historical process. To pick up a phrase I would like to return to later, we could say that the hope offered by messianic eschatology is the complete severance between truth and knowledge, which thereby necessitates a full wager in what Kierkegaard declared an otherwise absurd, or untimely, "leap of faith."

What does this mean? The eschatological hope suggests some event (that has already happened) to be the particular site of truth, and which is yet to fully reveal itself in time. It is a leap of faith to accept this past moment and hold fast to its promise moving forward. The danger is that fixing the location of the universal in such a normative, if not dogmatic, manner seems almost inevitably to beg the very subjective skepticism and possible cynicism it originally proposed to avoid. It is one thing to argue that every position is limited within our subjective understanding, that any claim to knowledge is actually at heart a faith-based claim, but if all claims are merely acts of faith, whatever are we to do other than fall into violence when faiths collide? We find ourselves to be subjects juxtaposed between faithfulness and futility, imprisoned as a stranger in a world without God (or with a distant God) but still charged with a divine commandment to sustain hope.

These messianic traditions are broadly translated into the modern secular vocabulary; take for instance Feuerbach's philosophy of human alienation. In his *Essence of Christianity*, Feuerbach argues for a "true or anthropological essence of religion" whereby God is understood to no longer be an actual metaphysical presence ("God is no longer anything more ... than a negative being") but the formal projection of the features and needs of humanity, especially the more virtuous aspects of our inner nature. "[God] is the principle of salvation, of good dispositions and actions, consequently [our] own good principles and nature."[103] In misrecognizing the anthropological character of the divine, Feuerbach argues that humanity becomes alienated from their divine potential to speak a more perfect social world into existence, and consequently ends up reproducing, or at least tacitly accepting, the irrationalities and imperfections of the current situation. Rather than despair, however, Feuerbach presents this realization as cause for celebration, for if perfection or non-alienation is not real, then imperfection would not have been experienced in the first place as imperfection. In other words, the failures of political (and personal) experience do not undermine the truth of our guiding claims and ideological values; quite the contrary, they constitute the actual proofs of their value and

103 Ludwig Feuerbach, *The Essence of Christianity* (originally published 1841, Prometheus Books 1989) Ch. 1, Sect. 2.

necessity, the surest guarantee that we are merely passing through a transitory stage to some more perfect realization of our divine capacities.[104] If the calling is not real, then why do we feel despair and guilt when we do not answer its appeal?

In more recent theories of international law and philosophy, this structure of messianic hope is translated directly from Feuerbach into support of the liberal cosmopolitan project as the universal site and sole metric of emancipatory politics.[105] First, liberal cosmopolitanism, like God, is emptied of any substantive or positive content to become "no longer anything more ... than a negative being" (Feuerbach), its universalism premised on remaining "empty, a negative instead of a positive claim" (Koskenniemi).[106] Second, this emptiness is itself the incarnation or formal embodiment of the ideal aspirations and nature of humanity. Thus, just as God is "nothing more than the representations of the powers of the human mind, expressed in the language of metaphor and hyperbole" (Feuerbach), international law represents the formal or "ideal relationship between free individuals and communities ... an aspiration of how the world might be, if only we were better" (Koskenniemi), an "idea of justice ... and an idea of democracy ... the formality of a structural messianism" (Derrida).[107] Collapsing the distinction between a Christian and secular practice of faith and politics, the 'internal morality' of international law therefore functions in striking similarity to the law of the Old Testament or the divine character of Christ, as the aesthetic (abstracted) standard against which initiates discover and measure their own aspirations and efforts, whereby

104 In relation to the Feuerbach analogy, I am particularly inspired by Rasulov, supra note 56.

105 "The modern international project builds its approach to the subject of international law's universality ... essentially ... is based ... [on] the Feuerbachian philosophy of human alienation ... Where Feuerbach speaks of the self-inflicted alienation of the human spirit, the dominant dogma of the modern international project speaks of international law's unrealized potential for universality ... Where Feuerbach speaks of a human essence transcending its own alienation by realizing its authentic potential for infinity, the dominant dogma speaks of the vindication of international law's universalist promise brought by the self-realization of legal universality secured by an intense self-reform of the international law field ... The tags and labels are different, but the underlying logic and landscape of ideas are essentially the same." Id.

106 Koskenniemi, supra note 99 at 504. This is what Koskenniemi calls a "culture of formalism," which he describes in the next sentence: "it tries to induce every particularity to bring about the universality hidden in it." Again, we confront that old formula: the universal inside the private, the public in the private, the universal in the particular, virtue through vice. For a brief discussion of this theme in international law, see John Haskell and Akbar Rasulov, supra note 56.

107 Jacques Derrida, *Spectres of Marx: The State of the Debt, the Work of Mourning and the New International* (originally published 1993, Routledge 1994) 59.

our failures merely testify to the transcendent (e.g., universal) essence of its promise:

> The law's internal morality ... [is] so many names for universality and so many opportunities for moral failure ... [but] without law, there would be no such scales. And without such scales ... life would be – well – livable but unlovely ... Law's failures, in this regard, only highlight the significance of its aspirations ...[108] [If] calling for such (continued) reform seems too mundane a conclusion in an age when even international lawyers are losing faith in the secular – well, it can always be redescribed in the messianic language of present imperfection merely highlighting the brightness of law's promise ... a self-correcting, secular project whose meaning would nonetheless be given by a horizon of transcendence ...[109] This is a messianic argument and a Christian vision. The fallibility of present society is taken for granted. So is the fallibility of the human beings that inhabit that society and the law they create out of their narrow vision. This is not a recipe for resignation, however, but rather a cause for joy and anticipation ... And the call for proselytism follows naturally: "The liberation has begun, but it does not yet engage the majority of the world's people."[110]

Within the Western tradition of political theology, the necessary and ineffable constitution of the universal, experienced as some irreducible or absent fullness (e.g., messianic promise), casts the international lawyer who adopts the not-All position in the role of the mystic. To publicly confess that the "liberation has begun" is to proclaim the glory of a return that has not yet happened but which merits our resolve and fidelity, to adopt the song of the night "watchmen" of the Old Testament:[111]

---

108 Martti Koskenniemi, "Formalism, Fragmentation, Freedom: Kantian Themes in Today's International Law" 4 *No Foundations* 7, 23 (2007).

109 Martti Koskenniemi, "International Law and Political Theology: How to read the Nomos der Erde?" 11:4 *Constellations* 492, 511 (2006).

110 Martti Koskenniemi, "Legal Cosmopolitanism: Tom Franck's Messianic World" 35 *New York University Journal of International Law and Politics* 471, 483–484 (2003). For a brief discussion around this quote, see Judith Grbich, "Secrets of the Fetish in International Law's Messianism" in Anne Orford (ed), *International Law and its Others* (Cambridge University Press 2009) 197, 203.

111 In this section, it is difficult to avoid the genderfication of language. I think being deliberate about gender word choices is not post-modern angst; choices carry significant ideological baggage. The choice to use gendered terms as much as I do in this section is to try and be faithful to the way the dialogue currently operates in the literature, and also to

How beautiful upon the mountain
Are the feet of him who brings good tidings,
Who publishes peace, who brings good tidings of good,
Who publishes salvation,
Who says to Zion, "Your God reigns."

Hark, your watchmen lift up their voice,
Together they sing for joy;
For eye to eye they see
The return of the Lord to Zion.[112]

The image of "the return of the Lord" over the mountains harkens back to Moses' description in Deuteronomy of the blessings of God given to sustain the Jewish people through the trials of their exodus in the desert:

The Lord came from Sinai,
And dawned from Se'ir upon us;
He shone forth from Mount Paran,
He came from the ten thousands of holy ones,
With flaming fire at his right hand.[113]

Yet the clarity of this moment is something that is remembered, the climax of a revelation that must be held on to against all odds:

The oracle concerning Dumah.
One is calling to me from Se'ir,
"Watchman, what of the night?
Watchman, what of the night?"

The watchman says:
"Morning comes, and also the night.
If you will inquire, inquire;
Come back again."[114]

---

highlight some of its weirdness. And of course, a nightwatchman could easily become a nightwatch-person, but this seems unnecessary and strips the text of a certain feel.

112 *Isaiah* 52:7–9 (Amplified Bible Classic Version).

113 *Deuteronomy* 33:2 (English Standard Version).

114 *Isaiah* 21:11–12 (English Standard Version).

As noted by the Protestant sociologist, Peter Berger, the literal translation from the Hebrew reads “the burden of Dumah,” the word “burden” signifying “the weight of an oracle directed against this or that object of God’s wrath.” Se’ir is a stretch of hills to the south-east of the Dead Sea, but Dumah appears not to be an actual location, its literal meaning “silence.” In this sense, the role of mystic as night watchman is to testify to the “burden of silence,” to remind us through the night that morning will come, but that it will depend on us to “inquire, inquire,” and to “come back again.”[115] By maintaining the openness to the sublime reality that grounds our political and spiritual existence, the night watchman initiates others into an unending effort to fill the void, to join in a song that can only be sung in the indeterminacy, or expectancy, of the morning. “If the mystical experience is really going to be the experience of an absolute transcendence, it must remain indeterminate,” explains Ernesto Laclau, “[And] like mystic fullness, political fullness needs to be named in terms deprived, as much as possible, of any positive content.”[116] The burden and the hope of the mystic, in other words, is the “poetics of the wait, of a threshold that cannot be crossed but must be maintained.”[117]

The threshold is the indeterminate, yet life-giving expression of incommensurable polarities that the mystic must mediate: reality (apology) – ideal (utopia), romantic pathos – nihilistic iconoclasm, finite (particular, substantive) – infinite (universal, formal), past (history) – future (policy), and so on. This conception of the mystic calling passes through Western intellectual professions: in the late 19th century, the “high art” of historiography; in the interwar period, poetry; in the Cold War era, a return to historical interpretation; and today, among other locations, international law. Speaking of the pleasure and costs of this mystic charge as a “mad love,” Andre Breton writes:

> At the forefront of discovery … from the moment when a certain learned man became convinced that he had witnessed a phenomenon, hitherto unknown, to the time when he began to measure the import of his observation – all feeling of duration abolished by the intoxicating atmosphere of chance – a very delicate flame highlights or perfects life’s meaning as nothing else can … Still today I am only counting on what comes of my own openness, my eagerness to wander in search of everything, which, I am confident, keeps me in mysterious communication with other open

115 Peter Berger, *A Far Glory: The Quest for Faith in an Age of Credulity* (Anchor Books 1992) 214–218.

116 Laclau, supra note 94 at 142.

117 See Badiou, supra note 65 at 24.

> beings, as if we were suddenly called to assemble. I would like my life to leave after it no other murmur than that of a watchman's song, of a song to while away the waiting. Independent of what happens and what does not happen, the wait itself is magnificent.[118]

Here we can see the "thesis of the stalk, or the wait" embodies the not-All paradox: on the one hand, in an almost masochistic register, the poet guardian can only keep hold of the real by remaining indifferent to what may or may not happen (e.g., to resist the phallic temptation to name the "All"); on the other hand, this intense indifference towards the particularities of nostalgia and suffering endows one with authority, the condition of human creativity/divinity (e.g., the life-affirming "not-All"). In a psychoanalytical register, authority (e.g., sexual desire) is conditioned on delaying its fullness (e.g., satisfaction). Translated into legal theory, the deferral of the cosmopolitan dream, as Koskenniemi explains, is the actual strength of international law claim to universalism/emancipation:

> Two notions of freedom are at play [in the formalist appeal of international law]: hubris and enlightenment. The former lives in strategic action [e.g., what Badiou calls "interpretation"] – the undetermined decision as the existential affirmation of oneself … immersion in the pleasure principle, pre-genital fixation and failure to reach maturity. The only thing that counts is distance from the mother's breast. But jouissance consummated is happiness destroyed; and you must move on to the next pleasure … freedom as enlightenment is about casting away that of your neighbour's and that if your jouissance is the only thing you pay attention to, well, then your neighbour will call in the police before the night is over. Freedom as enlightened judgment … [asks] what ought I to do in view of the justified claims others make on me . . That is a legal question … Freedom is the miracle of formalism.[119]

118 André Breton, *Mad Love* (originally published 1937, University of Nebraska Press 1987) 25.

119 Koskenniemi, supra note 109 at 25. The text I am quoting here is from the actual transcribed speech that served as the basis for the published version of the talk. The speech was uploaded to Koskenniemi's research site at the Erik Castrén Institute of International Law and Human Rights (ECI), and while similar, bears some interesting additions that disappear in the journal publication – for instance, the evocative line, "Freedom is the miracle of formalism." I have chosen not to provide the internet link to the paper as ECI is to be dissolved in Fall 2018 and it is unclear if the text will any longer be available.

However, the mystic challenge to act as the guardian of the community against any final consummation of the "All," is qualified by the necessity to still confront the unknown with some (albeit contingent) foundation. Drawing on German and American sources, historiography in the late 19th and mid-20th centuries strove to do exactly this by raising consciousness to the diversity and contradictions at the heart of human experience in history. For intellectuals in the aftermath of Hegel, such as Frederick Turner, the historian was not to interpret history in order to impose some intelligible pattern on the chaos of events (unlike a natural scientist) or discover an underlying essence beneath human affairs (unlike a theologian), but instead to construct narratives that allowed societies to experience themselves "as" (rather than "in") history – or in quasi-religious terminology, to enter into the mystic experience of endlessly re-enacting the moral act of creation.[120] In the post-WW2 era, the historian Leo Marx would be one of many to resuscitate this mythic vision of history as "high art," which might resolve the contradictory forces of human history in an idealized middle state, a "domesticated rural haven mediating urban civilization and howling wilderness."[121] As the historian Kevin Klein explains, this was essentially a modernized pastoral fantasy being offered with conscious political implications:

> In 1964, the year Marx's book rolled off the Oxford University press, the Free Speech Movement at Berkeley exploded onto national headlines and television screens. Atop a parked car, modern primitive Mario Save indicted the university for its complicity in the military-industrial complex and exhorted his fellow students to hurl their bodies against "the machine." Some did. By 1968 the wildness had spread ... Some academics joined in. Others saw civil disorder as the sad result of raising an entire generation in a bureaucratized mass culture. Humanists cultivated their own special fears, and some of these harmonized with Savio's pastoral manifesto. From the library, the auditorium, and the faculty lounge, besieged humanists peered out over the campus green and worried about evil machinery humming behind the well-financed doors ... [Marx's pastoral sought to clear] an Arcadian space ... [that] looked proletarian but wasn't. Scientific machine and humanist garden came together in a new academic middle state that saved a place for the democratizing force of

120 See Klein, supra note 57 at 1–128. This theme also runs through Peter Fitzpatrick's monograph, *The Mythology of Modern Law* (Routledge 1992).

121 Leo Marx, *The Machine in the Garden: Technology and the Pastoral Ideal in American* (Oxford University Press 1964).

> technology while identifying it with a more aristocratic order of great texts and their critical keepers. Content analysis sampled the daily lives of common folk, but only high art and the critical class that define and tended it could tell what it all meant.[122]

The ritualistic pieties and sacrifices to some charismatic phallic hero are rejected in favour of a canonization of scriptures (e.g., sources) and the need for a detached interpretative community. The positive transcendence of the utopian society in the future is replaced by a negative transcendence of victims and the politics of memory whereby the intellectual, like the mystic, stands guard in the threshold (the "middle state") to attempt and prevent the catastrophes and excesses of hegemonic struggles and desires:

> The process of reforms is a process of struggles ... [whereby] human abilities – new language games – are created ... Obviously a balance has to be established between antagonistic demands ... The balance consists of limiting the effects of both so that a sort of social equilibrium – something very different from a rational harmonization – can be reached ... [and] socially regulated and controlled.[123]

Labouring under the intense awareness of our expulsion from the Garden of Eden and the confusion of tongues at Babel, the mystic is forced to forsake any corpus of doctrines, institutions or other metaphysical foundations, and instead follow after an attitude, or tendency of mind, encoded across the surface of texts and layers of meaning passed down by past generations.

In recent decades, especially in relation to questions of political governance, international legal theorists and political philosophers have characterized their cosmopolitan projects in strikingly similar fashion, seeing themselves placed by history into a tradition that shares a mistrust toward politics and recourse to the decency of the guild, to "learn from [the] fathers and grandfathers in the profession."[124] What unites the mystic calling under so many names throughout the 20th century – the poet guardian, the night watcher, the stalker of the wait, the historian of the pastoral "middle state" and translator of the Weltgeist, the not-All philosophies in law and politics of the constitutive void – is the Christian tendency to descend into the Logos, to see language possessing a salvific power, of the Spirit incarnated as the Word, which may mediate the gap

122 Klein, supra note 57 at 234–235.

123 Laclau, supra note 99 at 115.

124 See Koskenniemi, supra note 100 at 4.

between the contradictions of human existence. The recourse to a "universal" vocabulary (especially carried out through the vehicle of law) that can manage cultural crisis and ideological antagonism is a long-standing trope in governance literature. From Hobbes' celebration of the arbitrariness of signs and the unbridgeable gap between words and things as the condition of an absolute and divine sovereign (established not by reason, but through faith and power) to Bacon's polemics for law as an artificial order of signs (that effectively represents and manages the affections of the human soul), philosophers in 17th century Britain translated the mystic awareness of the connection between words and desire into a formal interpretative rhetorical tradition of political decision-making, which passes through curious mutations into contemporary international legal theory. Like the mystics of the past, philosophers in international law today resist the desire to soil the sublime ineffability of the divine (e.g., by a direct "naming" of the particular site of the universal), but paradoxically, it is exactly by professing their radical awareness of the irreducible character of alterity in all things that international law regains its claim to universality, both as a political backdrop (entitled to universal application as a neutral, open field requiring a detached core of skilled practitioners) and, in a quasi-natural law register, as a reflection of the divine plan (no longer the embodiment of metaphysical substantive norms dictated by God, but nevertheless reflecting the divine, or natural, void that grounds all existence, and the logic of the divine creative process).

4 The Void in Context

The study of international law through the literary tradition of political theology reminds us that religious genealogies are still intimate to the legal imagination.[125] In some sense, we might say that Christianity is nothing but the practice of holding on to idols through the act of shattering their effigies –

125 There is a tradition of speaking about political theology in legal literature that is historical in orientation. The common suspicion pursued in this scholarship is that there is a productive intermingling of religious and secular dynamics in the development of contemporary Western modernity. The most famous example in this sub-genre is most likely Ernst Kantorowicz, *The King's Two Bodies* (originally published 1957, Princeton University Press 1998). I have chosen to pass over this literature because when authors in a historical vein of political theology and law are pushed, they seem to me to be grounded in the philosophical undercurrents discussed in our current study. It is not that historical study and mapping how it is being carried out is not valuable in itself (it is), but simply that my interest is in the more totalizing logic that runs through this literature and ties it to other disciplinary interests or professional agendas within the international law scene.

what Freudians might point to as an interiorization of the Father through the act of patricide.[126] The oscillations of faith, in religion or politics or law, are not roadmaps to understand the ups and downs of our march through history, but simply the structural logic of the political subject in the tradition of Western Christendom. Following this intuition, reading international law through a politico-theological register not only emphasizes its ongoing Christian heritage, but in doing so, provides a set of analytical tools to rethink argumentative logic within the discipline, and to demonstrate, perhaps only implicitly, that the various positions that international legal theorists have adopted over the course of the last century have occupied a strikingly parochial and narrow field of political and religious imagination. International legal arguments come from the same village, and their theoretical differences are most often the very stuff of family romance.[127]

Whether or not this is a bad thing is beside the point; my hunch is that it is an inescapable condition of our existence, just as our childhood is part of our past. If this is the case, then the professional rebellion against our past is just so many ways to deal, in political terms, with the nostalgia of imperialism and the underlying anxieties and traumas that come with this fading time. That this counsels nihilistic iconoclasm or absurd existential courage, however, is to miss the gift of the "return" of religion to the linguistic forefront of international law. I want to reflect briefly on the lessons of the phallic and feminine narratives, and then suggest the opening of a new politico-theological direction that is already underway, albeit nascent, in international legal theory.

The appeal of dividing international legal theory into a phallic and not-All logic is that it provides us an explanatory framework of what appears to be a distinctly European predicament (or set of conditions and desires) at the very nexus of religion, politics and law. First, the need to openly confess

126 See Sigmund Freud, *Moses and Monotheism* (originally published 1939, Random House 1955).

127 This seems a central lesson in literature identified as American Critical Legal Studies (CLS) and New Approaches to International Law (NAIL). Authors in these scenes are often criticized for over-emphasizing conceptual frameworks and linguistic play at the expense of sociological contexts (e.g., class, power). But, to some extent, this misses the point being made: what look like stark differences are actually just variations within a narrow ideational (and, most likely, ideological) spectrum, which in turn might lead scholars to be more circumspect in their self-understanding of what they are doing when they are teaching, writing, and so forth. If this is the case (and should be relatively obvious once revealed), its inability to 'sink in' with the academy in all its political colours raises the question, why? In this vein of inquiry, see Pierre Schlag, "Spam Jurisprudence, Air Law, and the Rank Anxiety of Nothing Happening (A Report on the State of the Art)" 97 *Georgetown Law Review* 803 (2009).

professional (and religious) complicity in the undeniable evils and butchery of our ancestors' imperialisms (e.g., colonialism, genocide, inter-European warfare). Second, the contemporary professional (and also very much political) commitment to protect international law's future from any return to this violent phallocentricity (thereby conceiving international law as a culture of formal restraint on power, promoting a liberal democratic attitude). And third, maintaining international law as the privileged medium of a new aesthetic that may give us some emancipatory, regenerative hope towards the future, which, with the return of religion to global governance, is able to maintain the positive components of a "secular" cosmopolitan lifestyle while also more openly acknowledge a hitherto marginalized spiritual dimension of political and personal existence. In other words, it rationalizes the failures and narrowness of international law; and not simply by means of apology, but as the actual proof that international law expresses the highest potential of organizational imagination for all humanity.[128] This narrative is the contemporary garb of the Protestant ethic in the service of global capitalism.[129]

4.1 *The Void in Context: Subjectivity*

The interpretive dissonance concerning the post-foundational tradition centres on two distinctly politico-theological axioms: first, concerning the nature of how the politico-religious subject is constituted and maintained, and second, the relationship between truth and knowledge. The purpose of this section is to explore the first case, concerning the conditions of the subject, where we will see the message within the literature is that the ideals formally encoded in international law and the practices of cosmopolitan democracy embody the core "essence" of humanity, and the failure to realize these ideals are not the fault of the ideals themselves but the fact that they exist within an imperfect, and often violent world. The underlying assumption of

128 This seems the target of Zoran Oklopcic's recent monograph, *Beyond the People: Social Imaginary and Constant Imagination* (Oxford University Press 2018).

129 Weber suggested that the tendencies we call capitalism were facilitated (rather than caused) by culturally specific historical conditions – namely Christianity, or more specifically, certain Protestant characteristics. In recent years, it is common to hear that there is no longer any necessary connection between capitalism and liberalism: capitalism is not a basis for liberalism, nor liberalism for capitalism. They do not lead to one another, nor is there any necessary link. Perhaps what is actually lamented, to some extent, is not that liberalism is disposable, but a certain white oriented Protestantism. If so, the capitalism we see today, what are its cultural – and specifically religious – conditions encouraging these directions? I will pick this up again in the conclusion. For an alternative reading that incorporates Weber, see Walter Benjamin, *Capitalism as Religion* (originally published 1921, Belknap Harvard Press 1996) 288.

the message is that the cosmopolitan international legal order offers a neutral and thereby inclusive field of political engagement where disparate agendas may be negotiated through peaceful if antagonistic deliberation. To put this more directly in post-foundational terminology, authors writing within the not-All tradition posit the cosmopolitan democratic model of governance as the concrete expression of an 'absent present', which is believed itself to be the natural pre-condition that enables the play of political contestation and identity, but conversely, is not itself captured within the antagonisms and contingencies of historical processes.[130] The challenge that emerges for cosmopolitan international lawyers is the trilateral call of the missionary – namely, to preserve the "purity" of its ideals from this-worldly corruptions (to focus on heavenly not earthly things), to preach inclusion (salvation) through the sincere effort to imitate this "pure being of the system" (to live "like Christ"), and to widen the spheres of its application to increasingly embrace longer chains of equivalences (the Pauline message that all are equal under God).

In my mind, this logic fundamentally mischaracterizes the nature of the political subject in a two-step reactionary defense of the status quo: first, abstracting cosmopolitan ideals from any "deep" structural criticism, adding up to an implicit act of "de-politicization," and second, projecting politics outward to both canonize the basic structure and logic of cosmopolitan democracy and naturalize the conception of a fallen world of power politics to explain when these ideals fail. This de-politicization commonly relies on ascribing some universalist "essence" or "experience" to humanity. To see this more clearly, we might begin by recalling the Feuerbach analogy in light of its criticism by Karl Marx in his *Theses on Feuerbach*:

> Feuerbach starts off from the fact of religious self-estrangement, of the duplication of the world into a religious, imaginary world, and a secular one. His work consists in resolving the religious world into its secular basis. He overlooks the fact that after completing this work, the chief thing still remains to be done. For the fact that the secular basis lifts off from itself and establishes itself in the clouds as an independent realm can only be explained by the inner strife and intrinsic contradictoriness of this secular basis ... Religion is precisely the devious acknowledgement of man through an intermediary ... [and the] failure to relate [these] fundamental concepts to the concrete situations and concrete activities out

130 As we have already witnessed, this "absent present" has gone through various manifestations across disciplines over the centuries: the mystic sublime, the poetic threshold, the philosophical void, the effect of "lack" in political theory, and so on.

> of which they grow and to which they must in some form or another be applied.[131]

For Marx, in other words, to bring religion "down to earth" by revealing that God was the distorted projection of human essence merely restated the alienating logic of Christianity in the figure of the "abstract rational individual." What Feuerbach did not realize, suggests Marx, is that this "human essence" did not actually correlate to some universal set of human traits or experiences which "could have been at any time and any place," but were in fact the production of a particular site of political struggle. This rationality was inevitably the philosophical expression of capitalism and the dominant class at that time to the extent that it successfully obfuscated its political coercion as the natural, ideal state of affairs in the minds of its political subjects. The civilized rationality that defined the contours of Feuerbach's "human essence" is echoed in the language of "balancing" and "social equilibrium" within international law, which presupposes that disparate cultures and experiences may be reduced to an abstract cosmopolitan subject. The purpose of international lawyers becomes, in the words of Chantal Mouffe, to uphold "liberal democracy … [as] the ideal type of a political form of society and not to the 'really existing' liberal democratic societies in their complexities," and in doing so "aims at the creation of unity … [and] attempt[s] to tame hostility and to defuse the potential antagonisms that exists in human relations."[132] In other words, the formal ideals of cosmopolitan international law now set the new bar to recognition as a political subject:

> [I]t underpins the historical process by evoking some quasi-transcendental limitation, some quasi-transcendental a priori that is not itself caught in the contingent historical process … [and] thus ultimately leads to the Kantian distinction between some formal a priori framework and its contingent shifting historical examples … an ahistorical a priori Prohibition or Limitation which circumscribes every political struggle in advance.[133]

131 See Karl Marx and Friedrich Engels, *The German Ideology* (originally published 1932, Martino Fine Books 2011) 570.

132 Chantal Mouffe, "Religion, Liberal Democracy, and Citizenship" in de Vries and Sullivan, supra note 3 at 321.

133 Zizek, supra note 53 at 109. This seems a more generalizable behavioural tick among scholars that identify across the political spectrum. In a variety of ways, authors often collapse historically discrete contexts into some underlying causal dynamic or conditional terrain to describe and explain things. It is not state friction but cultural antagonism; it is not cultural difference but class antagonism; it is this or that state entity rather than diverse

If we accept this political vision, international lawyers do not partake in partisan violence but seek to tame it as the neutral gatekeepers of the sublime indeterminacy that is called by the name liberal democracy. Of course, there is always the certain danger that political agendas or univocal reasoning will occasionally slip in to degrade the ineffability of the cosmopolitan ideals of international law, but this is exactly the calling of international lawyers, to tend the pastoral threshold, to sweep away any demand that might subvert the spirit of international law or push antagonisms too far.[134] The sin in cosmopolitanism's eye, in other words, is to propose any political project that might mount a serious challenge to the existing order on the basis that it will lead to the horrors of the Gulag and Holocaust – in more philosophical lingo, the crude phallic closure of the pure temporality of difference in favour of illusionary foundations:

> [T]he classical ideal of Revolution ... [involves] the idea that violence had to be directed towards a very specific end, which was to give a new

institutional fields and organizational tendencies. This is not to say that we should avoid positing explanatory frameworks, but too often it feels our methodological toolkits rely on relatively shallow intellectual work or a litany of relatively thin quotes and footnotes. For a discussion around some of these historiographic themes, see John D. Haskell, "The Choice of the Subject in Writing Histories of International Law" in Jean d'Aspremont, Tarcisio Gazzini, Andre Nollkaemper, and Wouter Werner (eds), *International Law as a Profession* (Cambridge University Press 2017) 244.

134 There is a tendency to separate law and power, even while acknowledging the politicalness of international law. "If international law has been degraded, it has also been violated," writes Bowring, in his appeal for what he characterizes as a Marxist re-reading of human rights. "[V]iolated to all appearances with its own full, enthusiastic participation ... Iraq, Serbia, and finally Afghanistan appear as three acts in a tragedy of intimate deception, a macabre vampire-bride relationship between law and power ... First, consummation, when law and power, freed by the end of the Cold War, seemed set for the longed-for happy alliance; second, seduction, when power sought from law invasion of its means of creation, international custom; third, rejection, when power, having taken and ravished the law, turned its back and walked away ... [Thus, it is] the vital importance for any serious theoretical and practical politics of defending the honor ... [of] the principles of contemporary international law and human rights ... International law contains within its principles and concepts the content of world-shaking movements ... the real, material weapons of offence and defense in the human fight for emancipation." See Bill Bowring, *The Degradation of the International Legal Order?: The Rehabilitation of Law and the Possibility of Politics* (Routledge 2008) 41, 208. If law is the product of imperialism, it is perceived to hold an emancipatory kernel at the heart of its project. A similar move, from critique to return, can be seen throughout most "critical" and "left" scholarship – for instance, in the third world approaches to international law literature. See John D. Haskell, "Trail-ing TWAIL: Arguments and Blind Spots in Third World Approaches to International Law" 27:2 *Canadian Journal of Law and Jurisprudence* 383 (2014).

> foundation to the social order. Now, from this point of view I am a reformist, not because my social aims are limited but simply because I do not believe that society has such a thing as a foundation ... Even the events which in the past have been called revolutions were only the over-determination of a multiplicity of reforms which cover vast aspects of society but by no means the totality of them. The idea of turning the whole society upside-down does not make any sense. (Which does not mean that many ugly things were not committed in the attempt to perform this impossible operation).[135]

The entire artifice of this logic here reveals itself to stand or fall on the answer to a single question: if the symbolic field of the political subject is necessarily structured around a central void or impossibility, what is the condition or coercive logic that maintains the void itself? If we recall the gendered binary for a moment, the feminine reading holds that the constitutive void is not a metaphysical essence, but the irreducible "effect of a lack" that occurs between or through the lines of a set of equivalences where the greater the multiplicity of the set, the broader and more open its character – what we have called to this point, the logic of "the Word" (e.g., the "empty" quality of international law's vocabulary as the very possibility of emancipatory politics). In its legal and political expression, intellectuals have subsequently claimed the formal ideals of cosmopolitan democracy to reflect this supposedly universal experience of human existence. One may enter in and be recognized by the international legal order only at the moment that the subjective recognition of the "other" is internalized. As a negative form of universalism, international law places the ideal model of cosmopolitan democracy outside of political struggle, as the fortunate, accidental happening of modern Western society upon the pre-human condition of all creation.

My hesitation towards this approach, despite its gentle temptations, is that it seeks to avoid the necessity of coercion and faith that grounds and sustains any system of governance. We cannot escape serving a master, and we cannot avoid coercion. We are always already coerced into an order that does not need to be so. Freedom is not from coercion, but to have clarity in how violence is appropriated and toward what ends; if we are democratic in orientation, freedom would thereby mean to be able to make more and better rather than less and fewer choices. But the point is that violence is always integral to freedom of action and thought. We can see this at work in the logic of the not-All, or in every day anecdotes, or in the Christian stories to date.

135 Laclau, supra note 99 at 114.

Authors within the not-All sensibility attack any open partisanship as rigid orthodoxy, the authoritarian closure to future emancipation or critical self-reflection. However, by romanticizing the practice of endless questioning, authors here risk instating new anxieties and consequently their own set of hypostases.[136] It seems to me ironic that this tradition critiques the phallic pre-disposition to name the "All" while implicitly doing the same in naming cosmopolitan democracy as the political representation of the "not-All" and donning it with an almost metaphysical status – as the membership card to legitimacy. And while often linked to more progressive gender theories, authors so often present the virtues of rulership in tune with a distinctly unreconstructed "womanly" sensibility: gentle, a good listener, at once patient and passionate. If we follow this path, we begin to view the power of law as a gentle civilizing influence on our most brutish instincts and our writing as manuals in polite workplace behaviour. If we are very lucky, the dream of the international legal academics becomes to perhaps have the opportunity to whisper in the ear of the prince ... All so terribly Victorian.

All of this is actually so far from our real lived experience. It is easy to forget that in our most materialist human beginning "is not the word, but the scream."[137] To wander for a moment anecdotally, consider childbirth as instructive in the inescapable violence of belonging. It is an act that constitutes a truly perennial experience for humans, and yet simultaneously defies our ability to reflect or remember. We only can partake in our births as an outsider far after the fact, and this chance to have survived dependent on the responsible care of others in a position of discretionary power. How often we collectively remember these stories with rose-coloured glasses. It is in fact a story whose origins are by no means gentle; it is a bloody, disjunctive cut that announces our entrance into the world. We emerge in a suffocating silence, ruptured from one system to another, unpredictably, the umbilical cord to our previous habitat severed, and immediately we are blinded, turned upside down, slapped, and in our first breath, we scream:

> In the beginning is the scream. We scream ... Faced with the mutilation of human lives by capitalism, a scream of sadness, a scream of horror, a scream of anger, a scream of refusal: NO ... The starting point of theoretical reflection is opposition, negativity, struggle. It is from rage that

136 Akbar Rasulov, "CLS and Marxism: a history of an affair" 5:4 *Transnational Legal Theory* 622, 621 (2014).

137 John Holloway, *Change the World Without Taking Power: The Meaning of Revolution Today* (Pluto Press 2002) 3.

> thought is born, not from the pose of reason, not from the reasoned-sitting-back-and-reflecting-on-the-mysteries-of-existence that is the conventional image of the thinker ... We start from negation, from dissonance. The dissonance can take many shapes. An inarticulate mumble of discontent, tears of frustration, a scream of rage, a confident roar. An unease, a confusion, a longing, a critical vibration.[138]

The scream of refusal is not simply a scream which "expresses" some lack that needs to be accommodated; it is a violent condemnation of some existing set of material conditions. In political terms, this would be a public declaration towards a perceived wrong that demands not inclusion, but just the opposite – refusal. I do not want to overdo this analogy, but as we move into an overly religious example (the establishment of the Jewish law by God at Mt. Sinai) I would like to hold onto three things: first, the violent, disruptive nature that introduces a new subject; second, the inability to anticipate the moment of rupture beforehand, as well as the impossibility to keep a faithful record of it afterward; and third, the immediacy of the scream in relation to its concrete conditions.

The Mt. Sinai account is found in the later passages of *Exodus*, the second book in the Pentateuch. The mainstream version of the story goes something like this ... Moses leads the slaves out of Egypt into the desert of Sinai, where God commands Moses to ascend the mountain and receive the commandments of God. When Moses returns from the mountain with the Ten Commandments, he finds the people have melted all their jewelry they brought from Egypt into the image of golden calf deity, and worship around it in drunken revelry. In anger, Moses smashes the stone tablets against the idol, grounds it into a fine dust and forces the people to consume it. Moses returns up the mountain, petitions God to save the people, and receives a new copy of commandments that the people declare they will fully obey, and in return they are again promised the land of Canaan as a blessing for being the chosen people of God. This is a reading in the not-All register: after hundreds of years of slavery, the people are finally convinced to leave the prior order to the emptiness of the desert (e.g., the void) whereby through the "Word" of the law they undergo the opening acts of ethno-national self-determination, united by a common covenant and an unfulfilled hope (e.g., the receding messianic hope of the promised land).

But this is the Sunday school version, sanitized of its violent and often bloody purges, which the law circles in unspoken anxiety: yes, we are united

138 Id.

as one, but only because those who dissented or broke rank are no longer with us, and let this be a lesson. "[G]radual pedagogy is a euphemistic description of the lesson Moses taught the people at the foot of the mountain," writes Michael Walzer, "[Rather it was] a lesson written in blood ... an absolutely crucial moment in the transition from house of bondage to promised land."[139] Upon descending the mountain and grounding the golden calf into powder for the people to drink, the text reads:

> Moses saw that the people were running wild and that Aaron had let them get out of control and so become a laughingstock to their enemies. So he stood at the entrance to the camp and said, "Whoever is for the Lord, come to me." And all the Levites rallied to him. Then he said to them, "This is what the Lord, the God of Israel, says: 'Each man strap a sword to his side. Go back and forth through the camp from one end to the other, each killing his brother and friend and neighbour.'" The Levites did as Moses commanded, and that day about three thousand of the people died. Then Moses said, "You have been set apart to the Lord today, for you were against your own sons and brothers, and he has blessed you this day."[140]

The danger of the cosmopolitan version to international law is that characterizing ideals as somehow formally empty or neutral suppresses their own exclusionary basis – exactly the critique that it levels upon the "All" logic of the phallus. It presents the Sunday school version of its history and development, sanitized of its (necessarily) irrational and violent origins. In psychoanalytic terms, the Lacanian Real: a trauma that gives shape to the argumentative and organizational infrastructure, but which the system cannot itself face up to.[141]

---

139 Michael Walzer, *Exodus and Revolution* (Basic Books 1985) 59.

140 These passages come from *Exodus* 32 (New International Version). To seal the legitimacy of the Levites' purge, the text tells us that God strikes the people a further time with a plague as payment of what they did with the calf, which harkens back to *Exodus* 20, when God warns the people as they venture into the desert, "[A]s I pleaded with your fathers in the wilderness ... so will I plead with you ... And I will cause you to pass under the rod, and I will bring you into the bond of the covenant: And I will purge out from among you ... them that transgress against me."

141 Let me be absolutely clear that looking to an Old Testament example offering a narrative about the early Jewish people is not meant to imply something exceptional or negative about Jewish people or Judaism. It is nothing more than a useful example when speaking about political theology in a Christian register. There is a bit of Stalin in St. Paul's recommendations found in *I Corinthians* 5, and the Western Protestant tradition is replete with its share of violent purifications and sacrifices. The same goes for just about any history

By denying the passionate, violent decisions that foster and maintain the governmentality of cosmopolitan "tolerance," the not-All logic reinstates the traditional power brokers and standing political binaries (e.g., universal/particular, tolerant/non-tolerant, flexible/dogmatic), and more importantly, routinizes a moral framework that projects its internal costs to the peripheries in an obscene cycle. Discounting the structural dynamics that lead to political failure, the reoccurring catastrophes of global politics are attributed to some outside agent or cause (even the inescapability of "human nature" itself), which is in fact a projection of the system's inner trauma. It is ironic that marginalized actors are offered membership into the political order upon conditions requiring an active forgetfulness or passivity to this very marginalization. To say this differently, the call to emancipation in this tradition is the opportunity to enlist oneself in the process of oppression that occasioned the original demand for justice and freedom.[142] Anne Orford makes exactly this point about the dominant practice of progressive legal ideology today in the context of religion and human rights:

> Legal texts justify intervention on the basis of the need to reject forms of nationalism that depend upon fundamentalism and religion, and to punish those who seek to found communities on violence, exclusion ... in the name of the law ... [However, that] with which we charge the other ... those fantasized communities ... in fact share that which the international community rejects as illegal: an originary violence ... is in fact the basis of the international community.[143]

4.2 *The Void in Context: Knowledge/Truth*

The second axiom of post-foundational thought in international law relates to the relationship between truth and knowledge. In a not-All reading, the loss of any metaphysical ground catches us in a seemingly inescapable Kantian subjectivity. International lawyers assume the twin role of mystic and scientist, at once charged with instilling a sense of the limits of finitude among

---

or tradition. If there was something that tied together humans, it would be this shared bloodshed. It is not by chance that the inspiration painting the "Three Studies for figures at the Base of a Crucifixion" by Francis Bacon was not only the "Isenheim Altarpiece" but the words of Aeschylus: "the reek of human blood smiles out at me."

142 "I know quite well you're not believers, right? But you are all the more conned, because even if you aren't believers ... you believe. I'm not saying that you assume it: it assumes you" Jacques Lacan, *Les non-dupes errent* (December 1973), audio recording available at http://www.radiolacan.com/en/topic/215/2.

143 See Orford, supra note 96 at 68.

warring hegemonic interests and also trusted to ever-refine and accumulate the tried and tested practices and beliefs of governance. The result in international law is a heightened sense of uncertainty towards "novel" political claims, even while we fine tune our legal instruments to the actual behaviours, beliefs and needs of previously marginalized groups. If truth exists, it is confined to the subjective space of individual experience or insular cultural traditions. In contrast to truth, knowledge as objective content accumulates through history, giving empirical insight into policy-making and interdisciplinary cost-benefit analysis. In other words, the ungrounding of any final truth casts shade on particular claims to truth except to the extent that any claim may be demonstrated through the existing international legal order. The claim is transferred from the realm of subjective truth or opinion to the supposedly neutral or naturalized terrain of knowledge. For the post-foundationalist in the not-All tradition, truth is consequently bracketed in favour of a politics of knowledge that counsels explanation over prescription, and ultimately requires international lawyers fall back on traditional (or at least, familiar) disciplinary practices and interpretations to legitimize their claims.[144] To put this in slightly more political terms, we could say that the orthodox regime of knowledge today always cuts the truth in two: between what is opinion and what is grounded in some form of reality, so that opinion is equated with political irrationality/illusion (and thereby, dangerous) and reality is equated with political tolerance/

144 A philosophical discussion in this register, about "all forms of wisdom" is addressed in Badiou, supra note 61 at 319. To find respite in the practices and sensibilities of "the profession" is echoed throughout international legal theory. As Pierre Schlag has demonstrated throughout his career, the argument is circular. An act or individual is claimed to be acting wayward, and this accusation is justified by pointing to the internal community's mentality and processes. But what now if there is disagreement as to the act, or the appropriate source, or the interpretative method relied upon? How to make a decision in the face of disagreement between what is inside and outside the circled wagons of the profession? Answers here tend to dissolve into "right reason," "you know it when you see it," and so forth – exactly the sort of unsatisfactory answer that led to a quasi-sociological response in the first place. See Schlag, supra note 15. The basic take away here is that this inward look doesn't really tell us too much; its role is purely strategic, a defensive move. That it is often undertaken in good faith is just a form of ideology at work and makes it all that more difficult to confront. And to hope that it might be intellectually confronted and overcome is putting a lot of faith in ideas moving history, of a cognitive revolution leading to profound institutional change, and that it is the substantive weight of arguments that carry the day. This seems to me highly suspicious, even if our bread and butter as legal academics. For discussion around this theme, see Akbar Rasulov, "New Approaches to International Law: Images of a Genealogy" in Jose Maria Beneyto and David Kennedy (eds), *New Approaches to International Law: The European and the American Experiences* (T.M.C. Asser Press 2012) 151.

pragmatism. Behind this decision over the location and management of the cut stands a privileged interpretive community that legitimize themselves as neutral (what we saw earlier in the mystic's "pleasure of the wait") and well-equipped (possessing the most sophisticated expertise). The art of international law, therefore, becomes locating moments of discordance, naming them out-of-place, and initiating a process of appropriation that encircles subjectivity in a marketplace imaginary:

> For if a vigorous ascending class is able to model history and the concepts of its speculation upon its force, this obviously is due to the fact that it hypostatizes its will into the integral affirmation of the wisdom of the world, and to dissenters it leaves only the place of the general denial, of radical discordance. And if, inversely, we are in a ruinous and thoughtless epoch, in the putrefaction of the selfsame place where we remain and from which no new political subject is the internal excluded or the placed excess, then the opposite temptations – resigning oneself to the course of the world, supposed to be necessary, or withdrawing from it completely ...[145] Capital demands a permanent creation of subjective and territorial identities in order for its principle of movement to homogenise its space of action; identities, moreover, that never demand anything but the right to be exposed in the same way as others to the uniform prerogatives of the market. The capitalist logic of the general equivalent and the identitarian and cultural logic of communities and minorities form an articulated whole.[146]

What becomes clearer now is that the ideological strength of the not-All is its capacity to enlist the subjectivist critique of radical ignorance (its inability to count the "All") as a front-line assault against any political project that might challenge the underlying co-ordinates that prop up the institutions, beliefs and distributional effects of liberal capitalism. What seems to me to get lost here is exactly the possibility of thinking international law as either a strategy or promise of emancipation. On the one hand, since any critique is required to articulate its challenge (or vision) within the linguistic/conceptual spectrum of the existing symbolic order, its content is rendered de facto superficial, and predictably will only present at best a circular reaffirmation or unveiling of the very same ideological and material apparatus it set out to attack in slightly

145 Alain Badiou, supra note 61 at 317.

146 Badiou, supra note 66 at 11; Stanislas Breton, *A Radical Philosophy of Saint Paul* (originally published 1988, Columbia University Press 2011).

modified form – what ends up being called "reform." There is room for appeal, not direct action. To enter into the rights and responsibilities of international law and be recognized as a politico-legal subject is conditioned on the voluntary forfeiture of one's ability to take personal responsibility for helping change the world, instead enlisted to play the role of bureaucrat.[147] To the extent that political opposition refuses to accept the existing conceptual terrain, its position is rendered perfunctorily irrational, incapable of dialogue, and posited to therefore necessitate "exceptional" measures to eradicate its threat. The irony of this not-All regime of subjectivist knowledge and its politics of opinion (perspective) and impasse (hesitation) is that it seeks to define itself based on a critique that plays out to be in fact the mirror of its own authoritarian logic.

To escape this trap – which is merely another name for the phallic logic in the service of capitalism cut loose of its cultural moorings – is to inverse the relationship between "truth" and "knowledge" in order that we might return to the politico-theological understanding found in the holy scriptures: that "truth" is the secret to our existence, the "ground" beneath our feet, and the direction of our politics. This understanding, its inversion of "knowledge" with the primacy of "truth" is already underway in recent legal scholarship, and draws upon a heterodox Catholic interpretation of the core message of Saint Paul. The question here is: what would a "politics of truth" look like for international law in light of Saint Paul's teachings? *What do we mean by a politics of truth?*

In his 2004 reflection on two decades of humanitarian legal activism, the international legal theorist, David Kennedy, calls upon humanitarians to make

147 For a general discussion around bureaucracy in our contemporary age, see Graeber, supra note 80. There is, however, an unspoken eroticism to bureaucracy, which is all so often anarchy, charisma and ad-hoc decisions. Living in relatively industrialized cosmopolitan environments – buying our food at chains, shopping in department stores, walking along well-lit roads with cash points and multiple lines of transport – we tend to forget that most of the world is governed by an everyday anarchy, to the extent it is the result of non-formalized but all-very-real arrangements between given communities. This is not only the case in the hinterlands of Moscow or the inner-city of Los Angeles, but inside the state embassies themselves, within their most formal bureaucratic offices. Purely anecdotal, but I have found there is an art to getting your work visa in only one visit to certain European embassies in London, which requires anticipated advances of paperwork, simultaneously demonstrating status and debasing yourself to the generosity of strangers, hand-wringing and contrition, all of which adds up to an official "making an exception." And the same ordeal with slight variations operating in American and British bureaucracies. Kafka was on to something in *The Trial* when Joseph K. discovers the magistrate's law books in the courtroom are actually collections of pornography.

their "yearnings real" through a "search for grace in governance."[148] This language of "grace" is a provocative word, and throughout his book, it reappears along with others, such as "hope," "faith" and "spirit" – words that are unmistakably pregnant with religious connotation. To hesitate on "grace" for a moment and not simply pass over it as rhetorical ornamentation, what does it mean? In the *Oxford Dictionary*, the first entries suggest some analogy to the classic not-All position: "elegance of movement," "courteous good will," and "attractive qualities or behaviour." The next entry, however, points to its Christian meaning – "the free and unearned favour of God" – found in the third chapter of *Romans* in the New Testament of the Christian Bible. Written by Paul, the text reads in full: "For there is no distinction, since all have sinned and fall short of the glory of God, by his grace they are justified as a gift, through the redemption which is in Christ Jesus."[149] Alain Badiou explains the importance of the verses:

> Dorean is a powerful word; it means "as a pure gift," "without cause," and even "in vain." There is for Paul an essential link between the "for all" of the universal and the "without cause" ... This is precisely what Paul calls grace: that which occurs without being couched in any predicate, that which is translegal, that which happens to everyone without an assignable reason. Grace is the opposite of the law insofar as it is what comes without being due ... for Paul, nothing is due. The salvation of the subject cannot take the form of a reward or wage. The subjectivity of faith is ... the granting of a gift, charisma ... This is a profound insight of Paul's ... [t]hat which founds a subject cannot be what is due to it ... If a truth is to surge forth eventually, it must be nondenumerable, impredicable, uncontrollable.[150]

For Paul, the concept of grace as a "gift without due" is therefore wholly incompatible with the politics of knowledge for on the one hand, it cannot have been earned, and on the other, it comes to us without warning. It is the unconditionality upon which it arrives that collapses the distinctions which had previously governed political identity; it is, quite simply, universal in its address and gives no deference to authority or tradition for its own sake. In Kennedy's version,

148 David Kennedy, *The Dark Sides of Virtue: reassessing international humanitarianism* (Princeton University Press 2004) xxvi.

149 *Romans* 3:23–25 (English Standard Version).

150 Badiou, supra note 61 at 76–77.

"grace" also denotes a rupture, or incommensurability with the past, and specifically the practices and verities of pedigree:

> [Narratives] reinforce the biases and blind spots in our mental map of the terrain on which we work. They deceive us with promises that humanitarianism will be achieved in the final days, if we work now in our own interest ... They reinforce an unwarranted faith in the upward humanitarian spiral of conversations about the legitimacy of government action carried on in our professional vocabularies ... We must unremember these stories, set them aside, demand evidence for their long-term promises ... Only by forgoing such stories can humanitarians come to live again in history, with all its contingency and possibility ... International humanitarianism could promise more – a heightened experience of freedom and responsibility, a profession committed to the human embrace of action, fallen from knowledge but poised for grace ... Forged in disenchantment ... Deciding – at once uncertain and responsible.[151]

To be "poised for grace" requires we "fall from knowledge" because knowledge donated to us through the past is the very obstacle to grace in that it leads us to idolatry, the useless worship of false images, the unwarranted faith in our professional vocabularies, promises and mental maps. This is not simply the passing of one set of practices or values for another, but rather the complete inversion of the symbolic order whereby grace reveals the "pretenses of justice" and paves "the way for apostasy, for heresy." To mix Lacan and Paul for a moment in our understanding of Kennedy, "grace" is the unexpected event of the inherent, but disavowed, structural limitation of a symbolic order come to light as a radical excess that cannot be counted and which thereby actualizes the destruction of the old order of knowledge. If a dispensation is constructed around a central truth that itself has no ultimate justification other than its very own enunciation, any new dispensation – with its own truth claim – will appear as folly or danger to those that do not accept its calling.

But even so, what does it mean when Kennedy tells us "we must act on faith, but hope for grace"? The conjunction of the word "but" is at first puzzling, since the conception of "faith" and "hope" are so often placed in close proximity to each other, denoting something possible in the future tense. This is made even more difficult by the fact that the sentence links faith with action, while grace is only to be hoped in. If grace is the event, or gift, that comes without being due, what does it mean "grace" is only something here that we "hope

151 Kennedy, supra note 148 at 353, 357.

for," and how can we reconcile this in the context of our earlier statement that "grace" is the site of the numinous disclosing its mystery? Here, we might again follow Badiou's reading of Paul – namely, that hope is not the name for some anticipation in an ideal future promise, but exactly what accompanies patience through an ideal, or perhaps more simply, the enduring fidelity that is the effect of a labour. If "grace" is the universal gift that allows for emancipation (e.g., the politics of the impossible) from the guilt of the law (e.g., the politics of the possible, knowledge, pragmatism, subjectivity), then hope is the tenacity, the consequence, the reward of this tenacity and which simultaneously sustains one's labour, connecting the subjective experience of fidelity to the universal (truth) it labours under.[152] Hope is a reward one receives for steadfast commitment in action to a truth. It is not a possession but a state of being.

But if hope is the force that is produced by and sustains fidelity to grace, Kennedy now makes a sharp distinction between Protestantism and Catholicism in relation to the function of "faith." In Protestantism, we are usually told, salvation is dependent on belief, not works:

> This righteousness of God ... apart from law ... comes through faith in Jesus Christ to all who believe. There is no difference, for all have sinned and fall short of the glory of God, and are justified freely by his grace through the redemption that came by Christ Jesus ... Now the wages of the worker are not credited as a gift, but as an obligation. However, to the one who does not work, but believes in Him who justifies the wicked, his faith is credited as righteous ... For if those who live by the Law are heirs, faith is useless and the promise is worthless, because the Law brings wrath. And where there is no law, there is no transgression. Therefore, the promise comes by faith, so that it may rest on grace and may be guaranteed ... not only to those who are of the Law, but also to those who are of the faith ... [A] man is not justified by works of the Law but by faith in Jesus Christ.[153]

In contrast, Catholicism teaches us that faith is not marked out through a sincerity of the heart, but rather sealed with a public declaration made through action:

152 Badiou, supra note 61 at 93–95.

153 *Romans* 3:21–26, 4:4–5, 14–16; *Galatians* 2: 16 (Berean Study Bible Version).

> The word is near you, in your mouth and in your heart, that is, the word of faith we are proclaiming: that if you confess with your mouth, "Jesus is Lord," and believe in your heart that God raised Him from the dead, you will be saved. For with your heart that you believe and are justified, and with your mouth you confess and are saved ...[154] For sin shall not be your master, because you are not under law, but under grace ... [W]hen you offer yourselves as obedient slaves, you are slaves to the one you obey ... But thanks be to God that, though you once were slaves to sin, you wholeheartedly obeyed the form of teaching to which you were committed. You have been set free from sin and have become slaves to righteousness ... For the wages of sin is death, but the gift of God is eternal life in Jesus Christ our Lord.[155]

How do we reconcile these two selections from the text and the denominational antagonism over their interpretation? In the Protestant reading, faith is juxtaposed against the idea of "works" to designate a sincere belief. It is unclear if actions are required. What is important to the Protestant is the emphasis on the "sinful" nature of the individual where only the most minimal agency is left over to activate salvation, the almost passive acceptance of the gift. Salvation remains purely a matter of grace from above, or at least not something where we can imagine ourselves an active participant. This faith is akin to what Kennedy laments as the twin practice of modern humanitarianism: a disavowal, or monasticism, from the war-tables of power, and a certainty in the progress of international law. The humanitarian, for Kennedy, operates much like the cosmopolitan mystic, trusting in the certainties of international law and attempting to guard the purity of its universalism from the corruption of power. The problem here for both Kennedy and Paul is that a passive faith forsakes the very emancipation that is embodied in the call of grace to faith (e.g., to die and rise with Christ, to imitate Christ and overcome the guilt of the law) and blunts our capacity to see that the law is not the end in itself but leads us to moments of reckoning (e.g., the "event," grace) that might fulfil and bring closure to the anxiety of the law. A passive faith creates a feedback loop where we oscillate between comfortable belief and bitter disenchantment, alienated from our own labor and condemned to legal convention. We might say that the Protestant humanitarian faith is the temptation to submit to an idolatry of the Word that absolves us of sin (e.g., the "dark sides"), but only at the price of abject

154 *Romans* 10:8–10 (Berean Study Bible Version).

155 *Romans* 6:14–18 (Berean Study Bible Version).

obedience to the realm of knowledge. We betray "grace" and, in so doing, lose the gift of freedom:

> Christianity raises the question of the relation that sons have to the Law ... The sending (birth) of the son names [a] rupture ... within History ... That it is the son, not the father, who is exemplary, enjoins us not to put our trust any longer in any discourse laying claim to the form of mastery ... For [Paul], Christian discourse can maintain fidelity to the son ... only ... through a sort of decline of the figure of the master ... [T]he Good News, comes down to this ... pure fidelity to the possibility opened by the event. It cannot, therefore, in any way ... fall under the remit of knowledge ... The apostle, who declares an unheard-of possibility, one dependent on an eventual grace, properly speaking knows nothing ... [It] emerges at that point where knowledge, be it empirical or conceptual, breaks down ... Paul does not hesitate to say: "Knowledge [gnosis] will disappear" [I Cor. 13:8].[156]

In contrast to Protestantism, the Catholic reading of faith emphasizes its active component, that belief is only made real through works. If belief is to take seriously the offer of the gift, a faith that occasions the truth of salvation requires we make an active, public declaration.

> Suppose a brother or sister is without clothes and daily food. If one of you tells him, "Go in peace; stay warm and well fed" but does not provide for his physical needs, what good is that? So too, faith by itself, if it is not complimented by action, is dead ... Show me your faith without deeds, and I will show you my faith by my deeds ... [A] man is justified by his deeds and not by faith alone ... As the body without the spirit is dead, so faith without deeds is dead.[157]

What the Protestant faith often misses is that the "not by works" refers to what occasions the gift, not the character of faith. Grace as a gift without precondition may only be activated through faith, which is nothing less than the material, worldly ordeal of struggling in fidelity to the truth offered by grace. Faith is the name for our escape – from alienation based in the knowledge (and guilt) of the law – into a new life through the militancy, or even enslavement, to the

156 Badiou, supra note 61 at 42–45.

157 *James* 2:15–26 (Berean Study Bible Version).

truth of grace.[158] To embrace the Catholic faith of Saint Paul, in other words, is to become a partisan to some illicit truth in the here and now. We can see something of this move in his 2006 book, *Of War and Law*, where Kennedy collapses the traditional distinctions between politics and law into the figure of the partisan humanitarian and describes the practice of international law as "an ethics of military violence." In language that borders on a Schmittian friend/enemy distinction and the phallic equation of (irrational/pre-legal) violence and freedom, Kennedy argues for a new humanitarian militancy:

> To use law is also to invoke violence, at least the violence that stands behind legal authority ... Law no longer stands outside violence, silent or prohibitive ... Wouldn't it be better to bring the ... political and military ... activities [of law] into the open [rather than hide behind] the boundaries ... Wouldn't a more stable peace be possible if we recognized the usefulness ... of war itself, placing [it] in a common framework of discussion? ... [As a] matter of professional ethics ... [to see] some kind of feedback loop between our ethical convictions and our use of force ... offers at once new opportunities for strategy ... and the exhilarating feeling of thinking rationally about the perverse and the forbidden. Moreover, it enlists us whether humanitarian or military professional, as strategic actors in the drama of war ... to embrace the exercise of power ... May the human freedom of responsible decision be the vocation of our politics.[159]

The strength of Kennedy's argument, in my mind, rests on three interlinked claims: first, the possibilities of emancipation and justice are open exactly to the degree international lawyers participate in truth as militant partisans; second, this posture will necessarily be viewed as heretical, an "apostasy" of "the perverse and the forbidden;" and third, to sustain such an "antiestablishment establishment" will require individual action and collective organization. To put this together, we might say that Kennedy intimates a new political subject of international law – the partisan militant humanitarian – which he recognizes will confound the existing pedigree of international law and demand its own political topography. For the conservative dispositions of international law proper, the "new man" of Kennedy's reflections is a provocative or at least

158 This is not that far removed from Erich Fromm's religious dialogue about being rather than having, to live concretely according to a clearly identified purpose. See Erich Fromm, *To Have or To Be?* (Harper and Row 1976).

159 Kennedy, supra note 11 at v, 22, 108, 109.

entertaining proposition, and suggests new ground to escape traditional platitudes and contemporary despair. At the same time, I believe that something has been lost (or not followed through to its conclusion) in Kennedy's translation of Saint Paul, which sinks his argument back into the legal traditions of restatement and renewal that he originally sought to circumvent.

If we recall, the "truth" for Paul (as for Lacan) is a "disavowed something:" a structuring principle which cannot be named within the existing symbolic order without disrupting the legitimacy of the system and bringing a total closure to the ideological and institutional apparatuses of the system in favour of some "new heaven and earth." Truth is therefore something that cannot be arrived at through the existing processes of knowledge and opinion, for it is exactly what cannot be counted, arriving on the scene as not simply irrational, but illicit. This is what Paul means in the first book of *Corinthians*, when he writes of the untimely and radical pregnancy of truth:

> Where is the wise man? Where is the scribe? Where is the philosopher of this age? Has not God made foolish the wisdom of the world? For since in the wisdom of God, the world through its wisdom did not know him, God was pleased through the foolishness of what was preached to save those who believe. Jews demand signs and Greeks search for wisdom, but we preach Christ crucified, a stumbling-block to Jews and foolishness to Gentiles, but to those who are called, both Jews and Greeks, Christ the power of God and the wisdom of God. For the foolishness of God is wiser than man's wisdom, and the weakness of God is stronger than man's strength ... Brothers, consider the time of your calling: Not many of you were wise by human standards; not many were powerful; not many were of noble birth. But God chose the foolish things of the world to shame the wise; God chose the weak things of the world to shame the strong. He chose the lowly and despised things of the world, and the things that are not, to nullify the things that are ...[160]

And this truth marks the individual an outcast to the existing world:

> Now it is required that those who have been given a trust must prove faithful. I care very little if I am judged by you or by any human court ... For it seems to me that God has put us apostles on display at the end of the procession, like men condemned to die in the arena. We have been made a spectacle to the whole universe, to angels as well as to human

160 *I Corinthians* 1:20–29 (Berean Study Bible Version).

> beings. We are fools for Christ, but you are so wise in Christ! We are weak, but you are strong! You are honored, we are dishonored! To this very hour we go hungry and thirsty, we are in rags, we are brutally treated, we are homeless. We work hard with our own hands. When we are cursed, we bless; when we are persecuted, we endure it; when we are slandered, we answer kindly. We have become the scum of the earth, the refuse of the world – right up to this moment.[161]

The divergence between Paul and Kennedy occurs at the site of "truth" that magnifies into an antagonism between the politics of the Real and the anxiety of restoration. For Paul, the "truth" is the name of the excess, of the disorder that structures an existing topography and which constitutes the opportunity to displace what exists and substantiate itself as the new order of meaning. To labor in the "truth" is to act completely outside the rational subjective determinations of the symbolic order, and thereby demands a full wager (e.g., courage, faith) since the "truth" and its advocates will undoubtedly be equated with some dangerous irrationality or chaos that must be suppressed at all costs. Since the "truth" is exactly that which cannot be spoken or thought under the symbolic order of the law, its justice is an experience or claim of "the impossible" – which being impossible is beyond all justification. Born of grace, the truth as the disorder to an existing dispensation comes as a call for justice in the here and now.[162] It cannot be justified; it demands to be either embraced or denied (close to the operation of Schmitt's friend/enemy). The truth of Paul, we can say, enacts the politics of the Real.

At first glance, the "truth" for Kennedy follows a similar set of structural axioms: "faith" is equated with action, "hope" is ordeal in the present, "grace" is the gift of something that brings life, and "truth" is ultimately "heresy" to the prevailing tradition. The "truth," Kennedy reveals, is that violence is the modality of politics, even the politics of justice and emancipation, whether it is expressed through humanitarian codes of law or military bombing campaigns. This "truth" performs its own version of flipping the ethical world of international law on its head: international law is not perverted by power, it is nothing but the function and reasoning of power, and we become authentic, moral participants to the extent we give up the false pieties that keep us from accepting that we participate in warfare. To do so allows us to circumvent the vulgar moralism and impotence that haunts humanitarian efforts:

161 *1 Corinthians* 4:2–13 (New International Version).

162 Derrida defines justice in this way, as "impatient, uncompromising, and unconditional." Derrida, supra note 107 at 37.

condemning sensationalist terrors (e.g., the Gulag, the Holocaust, 9/11) under the false dialectic of intolerance-tolerance, searching for principles that might somehow resolve conflicting passions, paying deference to those traditional legal sources of judgment.[163] For Kennedy, one must abandon such pieties if really intent on enacting one's humanitarian yearning for justice.[164] "Imagine instead a humanitarianism whose end was criticism, whose knowledge was critique ... [of] the pretenses of justice as it is ... [and] reminding us to ask again what justice requires," writes Kennedy, "[Such a humanitarianism] might develop our stamina for ambiguity and ambivalence ... invigorating our political life for heterodoxy."[165] The world is far too complex to form a "positive" foundation of politics, and therefore, humanitarians should advance a negative "sensibility" that stands in opposition to the arrogance of certainty, reminiscent of Foucault's politicalized intellectual – the "intermittent, tactical surveyor, who, in light of the incomprehensible plurality of struggles, is not him or herself partisan," but instead advances "a kind of tactical criticism."[166] Truth leaves the intellectual left with the task of balancing and weighing strategies and values in the face of inextricable opacity.[167]

---

163 Badiou, supra note 61 at 293–294. This is a classic problem raised by scholars associated with American Legal Realism and Critical Legal Studies. As Hohfeld pointed out long ago, every right or principle or value or rule is always matched with a countervailing right or principle or value or rule. The judge is required to balance these competing claims, which ultimately becomes a thing of discretion, of policy. Exactly what legal reasoning is supposed to guard against. And more often than not, between equal rights, force decides. See Duncan Kennedy, "The Critique of Rights in Critical Legal Studies" in Wendy Brown and Janet Halley (eds), *Left Legalism/Left Critique* (Duke University Press 2002) 178, 199–218.

164 This is speculative, but I feel that Kennedy's argument is closely complimented in theology by the work of Paul Tillich, especially *The Courage to Be* (Yale University Press 1952).

165 Kennedy, supra note 148 at 353.

166 See Alberto Toscano, "Partisan Thought" 17 *Historical Materialism* 159, 185 (2009) (quoting and analyzing Foucault).

167 This proposal is writ large across the American critical legal studies and new approaches to international law scenes. And, in my mind, it seems an ideal worth striving for. We are forever wanderers in a maze. But there are dark sides to this sensibility if taken as a mantra in all things. To really face up to its limitations, it would have to be historicized (something the "critical" tradition is often hesitant to venture). In the 1970s and 80s, Anglo-American and Western European university staff watched the collapse of left-oriented political parties, the breakdown of "meta" explanations to history and politics within expert circles, and capture of ideological vision by a cosmopolitan elite dream, more comfortable with a politics of conscience and identity than economic struggle as the basis of party solidarity (e.g., the 1972 Democratic Party platform). Within the cloisters of academia – at least among the social sciences and humanities industries – this would mean disciplinary sensibilities oriented to endlessly refining "context" and exploring intersubjective perspectives, and all of this situated within an institutional landscape

This, however, raises the question how we might measure our evaluations without returning to the existing topography? We seem to be reintroduced to the very fray we sought originally to escape. To put this in religious context, the announcement that violence is the modality of all political existence (including law) mirrors the message of John the Baptist that announces the coming of the Messiah. In both instances, the message is not yet itself the "truth," not the actual content of that promise, not the realized Messiah – it only harkens toward the truth. This is the difference between a false and real messianic justice, between following Mammon or Christ. The question remains to be answered, what is the substance of this truth? Or as Lenin put it, "Freedom – yes, but for WHOM? To do WHAT?"[168] The foregrounding of international law's bloody character only suggests the possibility of some truth. Showing that coercion is the inescapable companion to any governance model does not necessarily help us deliberate the preferred logic that will direct this coercion, what framework of appropriation to best guide any future structuring of distribution and production. At its worst, it all too easily falls back into a strategy of restoration anxiety.

In other words, what begins as a critique of systemic ideals ends up returning to the fold. The price of sustaining ambivalence and anxiety is exactly this

---

where oversight shifted from the professional guilds (e.g., academics concerned with status and reputation) to a managerial cadre (e.g., human resources and executive staff pushing market-oriented cyclical audits). Progressive legal academics would develop a philosophical tone of resistance, but more often than not, this spirit of resistance would fit the new managerial model: balancing interests and perspectives, highlighting blind spots, encouraging new thinking and experimentation, resisting accusations of being partisan or unrealistic. None of this held true for more conservative scholars (e.g., Samuel Huntington) or those academic disciplines that could brand themselves as firmly outside the humanities and social sciences (e.g., economists). For discussions around a number of these themes, see Barbara J. Keys, *Reclaiming American Virtue: The Human Rights Revolution of the 1970s* (Harvard University Press 2014); Power, supra note 80; John D. Haskell, "From Apology to Utopia's Conditions of Possibility" 29:3 *Leiden Journal of International Law* 667 (2016).

168 This does not lend itself to easy answers. Agency is the name for complex structural conditions condensed into identifiable movement; structural conditions embody diverse and often conflicting internal and external patterns held together by, at best, certain predictable but time-bound tendencies. For an introduction into this way of thinking, see Louis Althusser, *For Marx* (originally published 1965, Verso 2005); within an international law context, see Haskell, supra note 133. For myself, analyzing these problems began (and continue) with conversations and reading Akbar Rasulov, along with other fellow travelers in what appears a type of "structural" jurisprudence. There are a variety of ways this goes, but for a recent experiment in this general direction, see Justin Desautels-Stein, *The Jurisprudence of Style: A Structuralist History of American Pragmatism and Liberal Legal Thought* (Cambridge University Press 2018).

return of the "truth" to the existing order of knowledge, effectively rendering it incapable of its emancipatory promise. Since the ideals of cosmopolitan international law are themselves maintained as the standard of emancipation and justice, this de facto pragmatist orientation to truth ends up forcing us to be resigned to the existing course of the world in large part, leaving us without anything but what Badiou calls "an ethics of personal behaviour," or what Kennedy labels a professional "sensibility" or "posture" towards governance. What is lost is exactly the insight of how the immanent structure and logic of these ideals carry within themselves their own impossibility to achieve their promise, and which thereby merely reinstates a politics of deferral. The existing power struggles are condemned even as they are rationalized as endemic and beyond any drastic challenge.[169]

This is the fundamental divide, I believe, between liberal humanism and more radical regimes: not a struggle necessarily over the legitimacy of violence, but the urgency of the call for change.[170] If we accept the proposition that coercion is part of freedom and that life ultimately requires decisions about how to allocate violence, the question is not whether power is acceptable, but rather if a particular situation constitutes an emergency that demands a wager. In other words, to draw out the distinction between what on the one hand is open for pragmatic assessment and the weighing and balancing of positions, and on the other hand, what demands justice at any cost in the here and now. The ethical moment happens when we move to direct action. In the face of doubt, nevertheless ...

5 Conclusion

The aesthetic celebration of the ethos of the watchman actually ends up a conservative outlook that is structurally, theoretically and spiritually incapable of taking seriously the immediacy of suffering and oppression that

169 "Law ... honor[s] its roots in religion, from which it inherited the 'principles and values' of something as broad as the 'Judeo-Christian' tradition. Religion begins as a social force, is then transcended and cabined by a new international plane of ecumenical insistence on the prince's prerogatives, is transformed into a 'philosophy,' the naturalist antidote to an emerging positivism, and survives in our pragmatic century as a set of 'principles' guiding the practice of institutions ... Religion, reconfigured as a tradition ... rise[s] to its new role in the secular establishment ... remarkably consonant with enlightened upper-west-side thinking ... roughly correspond[ing] to our current world, shifted perhaps two or three inches to the left." See Kennedy, supra note 1 at 313.

170 See Celia Lynch, "Acting on Belief: Christian Perspectives on Suffering and Violence" 14:1 *Ethics and International Affairs* 83 (2006).

sustains the current global status quo.[171] In other words, we might abandon our pleasant humanist daydreams and ask how we might come to terms with Schmitt's friend/enemy distinction. Rather than attempt to deny its violent implications – for instance, in a Freudian turn from "wickedness" to "neurosis" or the post-Marxist retreat from political economy to recognition – how might we embrace the radical wager of past generations, and again accept the call to real, material struggle for a better world, however we might choose to imagine it?[172] This could be stated in quasi-liberal terms, for example, as the "fight against poverty," understanding the open antagonism in defining the term itself and the difficulties facing any efforts – but which would distinguish itself in the urgency it invests in the struggle. Adopted as an imperative, a mass party line that cuts through all equivocation to demand an immediate resolution at all cost, it radically repositions the structural co-ordinates of political existence as such. This is not nearly so foreign to our thinking as we might often admit, if we merely thought of the war against poverty on the existential terms of a personal struggle against cancer or an intruder threatening our family or, more broadly, a hostile army invading our cities and towns.

Or perhaps this is not our calling, a war on poverty. Maybe as a tactical point of contest it does not go far enough to the root of suffering. For myself, the crux of our frustration (or anger, anxiety, death drive, suffering) is imaginative and material. We know we are trapped in a world that does not need to be as it is and we struggle to seize the radical possibility of egalitarian experimentation and communion.[173] But whatever the case, we need to know a place where

---

171 See Badiou, supra note 65 and 66; Gustavo Gutierrez, *A Theology of Liberation: History, Politics, and Salvation* (originally published 1988, Orbis Books Maryknoll 2000).

172 In Rilke's poem "The Archaic Bust of Apollo," "his legendary head with eyes like ripening fruit" and "his torso … still suffused with brilliance from inside, like a lamp, in which his gaze, now turned low, glaives in all its power" demands "here there is no place that does not see you", the moment demanding "[y]ou must change your life." This is not too far from Bacon's reaction to "the reek of human blood smiles out at me." One cannot but change one's life; what looks to others as a leap of faith worthy of Kierkegaard, with all the madness that Saint Paul warned would come arm in arm with following after whatever truth knocks you off the donkey, is for you a necessity, the only response to what occurred. Or less romantically, what we are talking about is not simply the anecdotal one-off ethical decisions we are confronted with daily in all their ambiguity, but the challenge how to hold true to literary and philosophical principles in a world of darkness and temptation, to hold certain things as bright lines that define our life. This refrain is most salient, personally speaking, in the most unlikely of places – in the *Lemony Snicket* stories by Daniel Handler. Our hope is in concrete, purposeful action; not simply an attitude or ethos.

173 See David Graeber and David Wengrow, "How to change the course of human history (at least, the part that's already happened)" *Eurozine* (2 March 2018), available at https://www.eurozine.com/change-course-human-history/.

we stand, and whatever we choose, we embrace its immediacy and fullness. It might lead us to fight for a job guarantee along the lines of modern money theory.[174] Or it could follow the anarchist drive toward a debt jubilee and freedom from compulsory work.[175] Or it might mean fighting to cut dependence and planning according to the logic of economic growth.[176] Or perhaps something else which embodies all these propositions. Or something altogether different ...

My purpose in this text is not to develop what exactly this truth might be, but simply to explain why such an approach to truth is necessary and purposeful. A virtue of political theology talk in international law literature is that it can orient us toward a more active awareness that we serve masters and bow before ideas that are themselves not justifiable through simple well-educated reason or polite humanist ethics. And, in doing so, it connects us possibly a bit more closely with the mass cultures in which we live, especially in this era skeptical of experts and hungry for meaningful change – what we too often mischaracterize as a "post-truth" era. The scope of expertise in practice is always confined to what the broader population will allow.[177] If anything, our times call out for truth and are tired of knowledge that digs us only further into an unmanageable future. Our own experts and best ideas are very much part of what led us into the dire situation we find ourselves today. If the roads we followed brought us here, perhaps it is time to do things differently. What this might be is not necessarily overt, but our goal should be to understand what our collectively practiced object of devotion is and what it might be – in other words, to name our "religion."[178]

For myself, I tend to think that our object of devotion today – to the extent one can speak of something collectively shared – is mediated through a specific

174 At the heart of modern money theory is a truth all-too-commonly suppressed: the public, boundless nature of money. For an illuminating discussion of money's public character as the "unheard-of center", see Ferguson, supra note 70 at 1–66.

175 See André Gorz, *Critique of Economic Reason* (originally published 1988, Verso 1989).

176 See Nicholas Georgescu-Roegen, *The Entropy Law and the Economic Process* (originally published 1971, Harvard University Press 2014). "Growth for the sake of growth is the ideology of the cancer cell." Edward Abbey, "The Second Rape of the West" 22:12 *Playboy* A23 (1975).

177 For an example of this orientation toward populations rather than experts, see Jedidiah Kroncke, *The Futility of Law and Development: China and the Dangers of Exporting American Law* (Oxford University Press 2016).

178 Fromm, supra note 158 at 110. "To clarify, 'religion' as I use it here does not refer to a system that has anything necessarily to do with a concept of God or with idols or even to a system perceived as religion, but any group-shared system of thought and acting, that offers the individual a frame of orientation and an object of devotion. Indeed, in this broad sense of the word no culture of the past or present, and it seems no culture in the future, can be considered as not having a religion."

form of credit-debt relation that demands a particular form of obligation. In fact, any dispensation we live within operates according to this formula. In traditional Christianity, the wages of sin are death, and all people are born into the sin nature, into a debt. But Christ has provided a credit; through his death and resurrection we may be saved, our debt redeemed, death avoided and instead life beyond the ages. To partake in this gift, an obligation: to love God with all your heart, to pray without ceasing, to submit to the logos of the scriptures. And from this conceptual basis, authoritative structures emerge, rulership is made real. In our current day, that credit-debt relation is no longer sin and salvation through the authority of the Church or other Christian leadership per se, but runs through the logic of money, of capital. Our debt is of this world, in future present value and imposed with all the severity of the Inquisition. And it requires of us a form of praying without ceasing, of endless accumulation. And this calling a labor that seems to constantly require more toil, to take from us money's doppelgänger: time.[179]

Each dispensation comes with an unregulated space that requires a steward. Originally, the heavens mediated by the church, later the earthly frontier organized around the central administrative state – and today, the terrain of the psyche mediated by the market and its legion of experts servicing manufactured desire. External and internal factors depleted the fantasy inherent in the frontiers of the heaven and the earth: doctrinal debates among theologians, the Gutenberg printing press, the mechanical clock, the steam engine and cartography. Today also, the promise of our stewards and their governance regimes seem increasingly out of touch, the liberal defenses of the psyche looking more and more fragile to those older dispensations. While these three tired dispensations coil in unresolved tension with one another, the epistemologists of a new age remain immobile and out of sight.

Or even more troubling than a world with an uncertain future, perhaps we already live within a new dispensation. In Christianity, we witness a seemingly infinitely almighty and all-knowing being fall for his own creation, desiring of their admiration and love, so much so that this creator is willing to reassign into human form and fully immerse in their experience, even willing to accept betrayal, loneliness, suffering, and ultimately execution. The creation is so lowly in comparison to the creator, so incapable of mimicking or participating in sublime divinity; and yet it is this complete alienability that is in a way the very undoing of the divine to the extent that it is God that begins to fall in love

179 For a discussion built on this theme, see James Gleick, *Faster: The Acceleration of Just about Everything* (Random House 1999).

with humanity, to associate with the dramas of his creation.[180] In our days too, as creators of the new digital reality, perhaps we too have spoken into existence a creation that will transform us to its ends. The algorithms that we fashion to serve our fabricated desires and manifest our most unrestrained dreams, could it be that not only will they too dream, but that our dreams will be of their romances, that we will come to think like them, to wish that we might feel what they feel.[181] In the governing orthodoxy of our current day, the algorithm promises a world that no longer requires human labour. Could we not imagine a society with few humans, serviced by machine and loyal human automata, walking the untrammeled earth like Adams in the garden? What sort of brutal appropriation of life would such a new dispensation demand? What sort of great exterminations? Surely, most of us would not wish our names written in its ledger of salvation. This cannot be righteousness; this cannot be what it means to be human. This cannot be our answer to the gift of life.

And yet, a new dispensation is at hand, and to be born again will mean dying to this world. To be in the world but not of it.[182] Such a thing would not simply be a persuasive argument or an idea, but something that unites ultimately through experience. Truth is not of knowledge but experience; knowledge always follows truth.[183] Whatever this truth might be, it will not be justified through right reason but an intuitive hope born of common suffering and shared struggle. That my feelings here may adopt a distinctly American-oriented missionary spirit, seeing recourse in a "can-do" mantra against all odds ... well, so be it, I was born American into a deeply Christian family.[184] International law lacks any internal rationality or moral code, but it does offer a bureaucratic language of political struggle that can enact political decisions and provide an institutional platform for engaging our times. Maybe its community can be part of whatever is to come on the side of the good. Trained as a lawyer, perhaps I am overly romantic about the role law might take. If we were to play the odds, the safest bet is a tragic irony that does not invest too much in

180 "[H]ow much less a mortal, who is but a maggot – a human being, who is only a worm!" *Job* 25:6 (New International Version).

181 See Steven Millhauser, "The New Automaton Theatre" in *The Knife Thrower* (Random House 1999) 76, 94–96. For the development of this theme, and a seminal text in thinking through the conceptual orthodoxy of contemporary governance, see Philip Mirowski, *Machine Dreams: Economics Becomes a Cyborg Science* (Cambridge University Press 2002).

182 "I have given them your word, and the world has hated them because they are not of the world ... My prayer is not that you take them out of the world but that you protect them ..." *John* 17:14–15 (English Standard Version).

183 See Zoran, supra note 128.

184 See Kennedy, supra note 11.

humanity.[185] In our current moment, it seems that ever more people are prone to adopt this view. But my feeling is that we cannot be content with this cold comfort and allow our time to be a dream deferred.[186]

> [All together now:] Sez who?
> God help us ...[187]

---

185 See Robinson Jeffers, *The Double Axe* (originally published 1948, Liveright 1986). Jeffers referred to this as a sensibility of "inhumanism."

186 See Langston Hughes, *Harlem* (*"What happens to a dream deferred?"*) (originally published 1951, Random House 1990).

187 Leff, supra note 85 at 1249.

Bibliography

Abbey, Edward, "The Second Rape of the West" 22:12 *Playboy* A23 (1975).

Allott, Philip, "Review Essay Symposium: Allott's Eunomia and The Health of Nations Thinking Another World: This Cannot Be How the World Was Meant to Be" 16:2 *European Society of International Law* 255 (2004).

Anghie, Antony, *Imperialism, Sovereignty and the Making of International Law* (Cambridge University Press 2004).

Ansah, Tawia, "A Terrible Purity: International Law, Morality, Religion, Exclusion" 38:1 *Cornell International Law Journal* 9 (2005).

Årsheim, Helge and Pamela Slotte, *The Juridification of Religion* (Brill 2017).

Arvidsson, Matilda, Leila Brännström, and Panu Minkkinen (eds), *The Contemporary Relevance of Carl Schmitt: Law, Politics and Theology* (Routledge 2015).

d'Aspremont, Jean, *International Law as a Belief System* (Cambridge University Press 2018).

d'Aspremont, Jean, Tarcisio Gazzini, Andre Nollkaemper, and Wouter Werner (eds), *International Law as a Profession* (Cambridge University Press 2017).

Badiou, Alain, *St. Paul: The Foundation of Universalism* (Stanford University Press 2003).

Badiou, Alain, *The Century* (Polity Press 2007).

Badiou, Alain, *Theory of the Subject* (Continuum 2009).

Barthes, Roland, *Michelet* (University of California Press 1992).

Baty, Thomas, *International Law in Twilight* (Maruzen 1954).

Beneyto, Jose Maria and David Kennedy (eds), *New Approaches to International Law: The European and the American Experiences* (T.M.C. Asser Press 2012).

Benjamin, Walter, *Capitalism as Religion* (Belknap Harvard Press 1996).

Bennett, William, *Why We Fight: Moral Clarity and the War on Terrorism* (Doubleday 2003).

Berger, Peter, *A Far Glory: The Quest for Faith in an Age of Credulity* (Anchor Books 1992).

Berger, Peter, Grace Davie and Effie Fokas (eds), *Religious America, Secular Europe? A Theme and Variation* (Routledge 2008).

Berman, Harold, *Faith and Order: The Reconciliation of Law and Religion* (Scholars Press 1993).

Berman, Nathaniel, "Modernism, Nationalism, and the Rhetoric of Reconstruction" 4:2 *Yale Journal of Law and the Humanities* 351 (1992).

Berman, Nathaniel, "Legalizing Jerusalem or, Of Law, Fantasy, and Faith" 45 *Catholic University Law Review* 823 (1995–1996).

Berman, Nathaniel, *The Alchemy of Empire, or, of Power and Primitivism*, Inaugural Lecture of the School of Oriental and African Studies Centre for the study of Colonialism, Empire and International Law (February 2008).

Berman, Nathaniel, "The Sacred Conspiracy: Religion, Nationalism, and the Crisis of Internationalism" 25:1 *Leiden Journal of International Law* 9 (2012).
Bloom, Harold, *The Anxiety of Influence: A Theory of Poetry* (Oxford University Press 1973).
Boer, Roland, *Criticism of Religion: On Marxism and Theology, II* (Brill 2009).
Bowring, Bill, *The Degradation of the International Legal Order?: The Rehabilitation of Law and the Possibility of Politics* (Routledge 2008).
Breckman, William, "Between Disenchantment and Political Theology: French Post-Marxism and the Return of Religion" 94 *New German Critique* 72 (2005).
Breckman, Warren, *Marx, The Young Hegelians, and the Origins of Radical Social Theory* (Cambridge University Press 1999).
Breton, André, *Mad Love* (University of Nebraska Press 1987).
Breton, Stanislas, *A Radical Philosophy of Saint Paul* (Columbia University Press 2011).
Brown, Wendy and Janet Halley (eds), *Left Legalism/Left Critique* (Duke University Press 2002).
Butler, Judith, Ernesto Laclau, and Slavoj Žižek, *Contingency, Hegemony and Universality: Contemporary Dialogues on the Left* (Verso 2000).
Byrnes, Timothy and Peter Katzenstein (eds), *Religion in an Expanding Europe* (Cambridge University Press 2006).
Chiesa, Lorenzo, *Subjectivity and Otherness: A Philosophical Reading of Lacan* (MIT Press 2007).
Christofferson, Michael Scott, *French Intellectuals Against the Left: The Antitotalitarian Moment of the 1970s* (Berghahn Books 2004).
Clark, Elizabeth, *History, Theory, Text: Historians and the Linguistic Turn* (Harvard University Press 2004).
Connolly, William E., *Capitalism and Christianity: American Style* (Duke University Press 2008).
Danchin, Peter, "The Emergence and Structure of Religious Freedom in International Law Reconsidered" 23 *Journal of Law and Religion* 455 (2008).
Dawkins, Richard, *The God Delusion* (Transworld Publishers 2006).
Dean, Mitchell, "A Political Theology of World Order: Carl Schmitt's Nomos" 23:5 *Theory, Culture, and Society* 1 (2006).
Dennett, Daniel, *Breaking the Spell: Religion as a Natural Phenomenon* (Penguin Books 2006).
Derrida, Jacques, *Spectres of Marx: The State of the Debt, the Work of Mourning and the New International* (Routledge 1994).
Derrida, Jacques, *The Politics of Friendship* (Verso 2005).
Desan, Christine, *Making Money: Coin, Currency, and the Coming of Capitalism* (Oxford University Press 2014).

Desautels-Stein, Justin, *The Jurisprudence of Style: A Structuralist History of American Pragmatism and Liberal Legal Thought* (Cambridge University Press 2018).

Erikson, Erik, *Childhood and Society* (Imago Publishing 1951).

Erikson, Erik, *Insight and Responsibility* (Norton and Company 1964).

Falk, Richard, *Religion and Humane Global Governance* (Palgrave Macmillan 2001).

Ferguson, Scott, *Declarations of Dependence: Money, Aesthetics, and the Politics of Care* (University of Nebraska Press 2018).

Feuerbach, Ludwig, *The Essence of Christianity* (Prometheus Books 1989).

Foucault, Michel, *The Birth of Biopolitics: Lectures at the College de France 1978–1979* (Palgrave Macmillan 2008).

Franck, Jerome, *Law and the Modern Mind* (Stevens & Sons 1949).

Freud, Sigmund, *Moses and Monotheism* (Random House 1955).

Fromm, Erich, *To Have or To Be?* (Harper and Row 1976).

Georgescu-Roegen, Nicholas, *The Entropy Law and the Economic Process* (Harvard University Press 2014).

Gibson, William, *Neuromancer* (Ace Books 1984).

Gillam, Terry, *Brazil* (1985).

Gleick, James, *Faster: The Acceleration of Just About Everything* (Random House 1999).

Le Goff, Jacques, *Time, Work, and Culture in the Middle Ages* (University of Chicago Press 1980).

Gorz, André, *Critique of Economic Reason* (Verso 1989).

Gray, John, *Black Mass: Apocalyptic Religion and the Death of Utopia* (Penguin Books 2006).

Graeber, David, *Debt: The First 5,000 Years* (Melville House 2011).

Graeber, David, *The Utopia of Rules: On Technology, Stupidity and the Secret Joys of Bureaucracy* (First Melville House 2015).

Graeber, David and David Wengrow, "How to change the course of human history (at least, the part that's already happened)" *Eurozine* (2 March 2018), available at https://www.eurozine.com/change-course-human-history/.

Gutierrez, Gustavo, *A Theology of Liberation: History, Politics, and Salvation* (Orbis Books Maryknoll 2000).

Habermas, Jürgen and Joseph Ratzinger, *The Dialectics of Secularisation: On Reason and Religion* (Igatius Press 2005).

Haskell, John D., "From Apology to Utopia's Conditions of Possibility" 29:3 *Leiden Journal of International Law* 667 (2016).

Haskell, John D., "Trail-ing TWAIL: Arguments and Blind Spots in Third World Approaches to International Law" 27:2 *Canadian Journal of Law and Jurisprudence* 383 (2014).

Haskell, John and Akbar Rasulov, "International Law and the Turn to Political Economy" 31:2 *Leiden Journal of International Law* 243 (2018).

Holloway, John, *Change the World Without Taking Power: The Meaning of Revolution Today* (Pluto Press 2002).

Hughes, Langston, *Harlem ("What happens to a dream deferred?")* (Random House 1990).

Huntington, Samuel, *The Clash of Civilisations and the Remaking of World Order* (Simon and Schuster 1996).

Huntington, Samuel, *Who We Are: The Challenges to America's National Identity* (Simon and Schuster 2004).

Hutchison, William and Hartmutt Lehmann (eds), *Many are Chosen: Divine Election and Western Nationalism* (Fortress Press 1994).

Janis, Mark and Carolyn Evans (eds), *Religion and International Law* (Kluwer 1999).

Jardine, Alice, 'Gynesis' 12 *Diacritics* 54 (1982).

Jeffers, Robinson, *The Double Axe* (Liveright 1986).

Johnson v. McIntosh, 21 U.S. (8 Wheat.) 543 (1823).

Kafka, Franz, *The Trial* (Schocken Books 1999).

Kahn, Paul, *A Political Theology for a Civil Religion*, Lecture at European University Institute Robert Schuman Centre for Advanced Studies (January 2012), available at https://www.scribd.com/document/211539197/A-Political-Theology-for-a-Civil-Religion-Paul-Kahn.

Kantorowicz, Ernst, *The King's Two Bodies* (Princeton University Press 1998).

Kennedy, David, "When Renewal Repeats: Thinking Against the Box" 32 *New York Journal of International Law and Politics* 335 (2000).

Kennedy, David, *The Dark Sides of Virtue: reassessing international humanitarianism* (Princeton University Press 2004).

Kennedy, David, *Of War and Law* (Princeton University Press 2006).

Kennedy, Duncan, "American Constitutionalism as Civil Religion: Notes of an Atheist" 19 *Nova Law Review* 909 (1995).

Keys, Barbara J., *Reclaiming American Virtue: The Human Rights Revolution of the 1970s* (Harvard University Press 2014).

Kierkegaard, Soren, *Repetition* (Princeton University Press 1983).

Klein, Kerwin Lee, *Frontiers of Historical Imagination: Narrating the European Conquest of Native America, 1890–1990* (University of California Press 1997).

Kohn, Hans, *The Idea of Nationalism: A Study in its Origins and Background* (Macmillan 1944).

Koskenniemi, Martti, "Formalism, Fragmentation, Freedom: Kantian Themes in Today's International Law" 4 *No Foundations* 7 (2007).

Koskenniemi, Martti, Mónica García-Salmones Rovira and Paolo Amorosa (eds), *International Law and Religion: Historical and Contemporary Perspectives* (Oxford University Press 2018).

Koskenniemi, Martti, "International Law as Political Theology: How to read the Nomos der Erde?" 11:4 *Constellations* 492 (2006).

Koskenniemi, Martti, "Legal Cosmopolitanism: Tom Franck's Messianic World" 35 *New York University Journal of International Law and Politics* 471 (2003).

Koskenniemi, Martti, *The Gentle Civilizer of Nations: The Rise and Fall of International Law, 1870–1960* (Cambridge University Press 2004).

Koskenniemi, Martti, "The Police in the Temple: Order, Justice and the UN: A Dialectical View" 6 *European Journal of International Law* 25 (2004).

Koskenniemi, Martti, "The Lady Doth Protest Too Much: Kosovo and the Turn To Ethics in International Law" 65:2 *Modern Law Review* 159 (2002).

Kroncke, Jedidiah, *The Futility of Law and Development: China and the Dangers of Exporting American Law* (Oxford University Press 2016).

Lacan, Jacques, *Les non-dupes errent* (December 1973), audio recording available at http://www.radiolacan.com/en/topic/215/2.

Laclau, Ernesto, *Emancipation(s)* (Verso 1996).

Leach, William, *Land of Desire: Merchants, Power, and the Rise of a New American Culture* (Random House 1993).

Lee, Grace, "David Lynch: The Treachery of Language," available at https://www.youtube.com/watch?time_continue=639&v=ffllV6-aqWU.

Leff, Arthur A., "Unspeakable Ethics, Unnatural Law" 6 *Duke Law Journal* 1229 (1979).

Leff, Gordon, *Heresy in the Later Middle Ages: The Relation of Heterodoxy to Dissent: 1250–1450*, 2 vols. (Manchester University Press 1967).

Limon, John, *Writing After War: American War Fiction from Realism to Postmodernism* (Oxford University Press 1994).

Lynch, Celia, "Acting on Belief: Christian Perspectives on Suffering and Violence" 14:1 *Ethics and International Affairs* 83 (2006).

MacLean, Nancy, *Democracy in Chains: The Deep History of the Radical Right's Stealth Plan for America* (Viking Press 2017).

Maher, Bill, *Religulous* (2008).

Mamet, David, *Writing in Restaurants* (Penguin 1987).

Marchart, Oliver, *Post-Foundational Political Thought: Political Difference in Nancy, Lefort, Badiou and Laclau* (Edinburgh University Press 2007).

Marcuse, Herbert, *One Dimensional Man* (Routledge 2002).

Marx, Karl and Friedrich Engels, *The German Ideology* (Martino Fine Books 2011).

Marx, Leo, *The Machine in the Garden: Technology and the Pastoral Ideal in American* (Oxford University Press 1964).

McCormick, John P., "Political Theory and Political Theology: The Second Wave of Carl Schmitt in English" 26:6 *Political Theory* 830 (1998).

McVicar, Michael, *Christian Reconstruction: R.J. Rushdoony and American Religious Conservatism* (University of North Carolina Press 2015).
Miéville, China, *Between Equal Rights: A Marxist Theory of International Law* (Brill 2005).
Millhauser, Steven, *The Knife Thrower* (Random House 1999).
Mirowski, Philip, *Machine Dreams: Economics Becomes a Cyborg Science* (Cambridge University Press 2002).
Moreton, Bethany, *To Serve God and Wal-Mart: The Making of the Christian Free Enterprise* (Harvard University Press 2009).
Muldoon, James, *Popes, Lawyers and Infidels: The Church and the Non-Christian World, 1250–1500* (University of Pennsylvania Press 1979).
Nye, Russell, *The Almost Chosen People* (Michigan State University Press 1966).
Oklopcic, Zoran, *Beyond the People: Social Imaginary and Constant Imagination* (Oxford University Press 2018).
Orford, Anne, *Reading Humanitarian Intervention: Human Rights and the Use of Force in International Law* (Cambridge University Press 2003).
Orford, Anne (ed), *International Law and its Others* (Cambridge University Press 2009).
Özsu, Umut, *Formalizing Displacement: International Law and Population Transfers* (Oxford University Press 2015).
Paz, Reut, *A Gateway between a Distant God and a Cruel World: The Contribution of Jewish German-Speaking Scholars to International Law* (Brill 2012).
Pink Floyd, *The Wall* (1979).
Power, Michael, *The Audit Society: Rituals of Verification* (Oxford University Press 1997).
Rasulov, Akbar, "CLS and Marxism: a history of an affair" 5:4 *Transnational Legal Theory* 622, 621 (2014).
Rasulov, Akbar, *Universality and the Ruses of the International Law Reason: A Tale of Two Scandals*, Lecture at the International University College of Turin Institute for Political Economy and Law Seminar Series (March 2011), available at https://www.youtube.com/watch?v=zToDR1jVqAU.
Rasulov, Akbar, "Writing about empire: remarks on the logic of a discourse" 23:2 *Leiden Journal of International Law* 449 (2010).
Robert, John, "The 'Returns to Religion:' Messianism, Christianity and the Revolutionary Tradition. Part II: The Pauline Tradition" 16 *Historical Materialism* 77 (2008).
Roberts, John, "The 'Returns to Religion:' Messianism, Christianity and the Revolutionary Tradition. Part I: Wakefulness to the Future" 16 *Historical Materialism* 59 (2008).
Schlag, Pierre, "Law as a Continuation of God by Other Means" 85 *California Law Review* 427 (1997).
Schlag, Pierre, "Spam Jurisprudence, Air Law, and the Rank Anxiety of Nothing Happening (A Report on the State of the Art)" 97 *Georgetown Law Review* 803 (2009).

Schlag, Pierre, *The Enchantment of Reason* (Duke University Press 1998).

Schmitt, Carl, "Appropriation/Distribution/Production: Toward a Proper Formulation of Basic Questions of any Social and Economic Order" 95 *Telos* 52 (1993).

Schmitt, Carl, *The Nomos of the Earth in the International Law of the Jus Publicum Europaeum* (Telos 2003).

Schmitt, Carl, *Political Theology: Four Chapters on the Concept of Sovereignty* (University of Chicago Press 2006).

Sewell, Bevan, "Pragmatism, Religion, and John Foster Dulles's Embrace of Christian Internationalism in the 1930s" 41:4 *Diplomatic History* 799 (2017).

Smith, James, *The Idea Brokers: Think Tanks and the Rise of the New Policy Elite* (Free Press 1991).

Stephenson, Neal, *Snow Crash* (Bantam Books 1992).

Strauss, Leo, *Natural Right and History* (University of Chicago Press 1953).

Strauss, Leo, "On the Interpretation of Genesis" 21:1 *L'Homme* 5 (1981).

Strong, Josiah, *Our Country: Its Possible Future and Its Present Crisis* (The American Home Missionary Society 1885).

Taubes, Jacob, *To Carl Schmitt: Letters and Reflections* (Cambridge University Press 2013).

Tierney, Brian, *The Idea of Natural Rights: Studies of Natural Rights, Natural Law and Church Law, 1150–1625* (Scholars Press 1997).

Tillich, Paul, *The Courage to Be* (Yale University Press 1952).

Toscano, Alberto, "Beyond Abstraction: Marx and the Critique of the Critique of Religion" 18:1 *Historical Materialism* 3 (2010).

Toscano, Alberto, "Fanaticism: A Brief History of the Concept" *Eurozine* (December 2006), available at http://www.eurozine.com/articles/2006-12-07-toscano-en.html.

Toscano, Alberto, "Partisan Thought" 17 *Historical Materialism* 159 (2009).

Twain, Mark, *A Connecticut Yankee in King Arthur's Court* (Oxford University Press 1997).

Unger, Roberto Mangabeira, *Social Theory: Its situation and its task* (Verso 2004).

Verne, Jules, *Around the World in 80 Days* (Oxford University Press 1995).

Viner, Jacob, *The Role of Providence in the Social Order: An Essay in Intellectual History* (Princeton University Press 1976).

de Vries, Hent and Lawrence Sullivan, *Political Theologies: Public Religions in a Post-Secular World* (Fordam University Press 2006).

Walzer, Michael, *Exodus and Revolution* (Basic Books 1985).

Watzlawick, Paul, Janet Beavin Bavelas, and Don Jackson, *Pragmatics of Human Communication: A Study of Interactional Patterns, Pathologies and Paradoxes* (W.W. Norton 1967).

Weiler, Joseph, "Europe in Crisis – On Political Messianism, Legitimacy and the Rule of Law" *Singapore Journal of Legal Studies* 248 (2012).

Witte, John, Jr., *Religion and Law*, Interview on University of California Television Conversations with History (August 2011), available at https://www.youtube.com/watch?v=W5glYC_topE.

Wray, Randall L., *Modern Money Theory: A Primer on Macroeconomics for Sovereign Monetary Systems* (Palgrave Macmillan 2011).

Wright, Will, *The Wild West: The Mythical Cowboy and Social Theory* (Sage Publications 2001).

Žižek, Slavoj, Eric L. Santner, and Kenneth Reinhard, *The Neighbour: Three Inquiries in Political Theology* (University of Chicago Press 2005).

www.ingramcontent.com/pod-product-compliance
Lightning Source LLC
Chambersburg PA
CBHW031331230926
51848CB00001B/179
9789004382503